Advance Praise

"We can't be the best version of ourselves unless we show up every day and practice. Rob's idea to 'do nothing' provides clear guidance on how we can accomplish excellence as leaders."

—MARK BERTOLINI, CHAIRMAN AND CEO OF AETNA

*"I have always believed in a balanced life. I believe people should work no greater than forty hours a week so they can have time to enjoy all the possibilities outside of work. It's not easy. It requires discipline, courage, and practice. Rob Dubé's book do**nothing**: 'the most rewarding leadership challenge you will ever take' is a guide to help you get there by 'learning to be truly aware and present.'"*

—JACK STACK, CEO OF SRC HOLDINGS CORPORATION

*"Looking to make your life more rewarding? Improve your leadership effectiveness? Reduce mistakes and increase your sense of well-being? Cut down turnover and improve staff satisfaction? The answers to all of these, and more, are right in Rob Dubé's wonderful new book. do**nothing** details the benefits of meditation, gets you started on how to do it, and shares very down-to-earth tips on how to stick with it. This book is guaranteed to leave you wondering why you've waited so long to start!"*

—ARI WEINZWEIG, CO-OWNER AND FOUNDING PARTNER
OF THE ZINGERMAN'S COMMUNITY OF BUSINESSES

"For many years, I've encouraged entrepreneurs to 'stay focused and don't get distracted by shiny stuff.' Easier said than done! Rob's book provides compelling reasons and simple instruction to take on a meditation practice—a practical life tool that allows for focus to more easily occur. After reading the book, I was inspired to start a practice of my own."

—GINO WICKMAN, FOUNDER OF THE ENTREPREURIAL OPERATING SYSTEM AND BEST-SELLING AUTHOR OF *TRACTION*

"For those Type A's like me who considered practices like meditation a bunch of hooey, all you need to do is read Rob's genuine and personal story to realize that doing 'nothing' can be a valuable key to success both in business and in life. His account is short, practical, and authentic—it will have you focusing on your breath in no time."

—PAUL SPIEGELMAN, CEO OF THE SMALL GIANTS COMMUNITY AND BEST-SELLING AUTHOR OF *WHY IS EVERYONE SMILING?* AND *PATIENTS COME SECOND*

"Many of the best leaders I know have one thing in common— they care deeply about their people. In our fast-paced world, being fully present takes practice. Rob's book, do**nothing**, simply and concisely outlines the discipline we can create to improve that skill. After all, in the end, what matters most in life is the depth of our relationships and the sheer number of people we've helped along the way. These represent true measures of wealth."

—VERNE HARNISH, FOUNDER OF ENTREPRENEURS' ORGANIZATION (EO) AND AUTHOR OF *SCALING UP*

"*I believe as leaders of our organizations—or leaders of anything for that matter—the ceiling of the organizations we lead are limited to the ceiling and personal growth of the leader who is out in front of them. After reading do**nothing**, I realize this book holds a new and exciting key to this essential personal growth. The why and how of a daily meditation practice and making time for an annual silent retreat is one of the many gifts of this book!*"

—NICK SARILLO, CEO OF NICK'S PIZZA & PUB AND OF THE NICK'S U, AUTHOR OF *A SLICE OF THE PIE*, AND NAMED ONE OF *FORBES* MAGAZINE'S TOP 25 SMALL GIANTS: AMERICA'S BEST SMALL COMPANIES IN 2017

"*Rob Dubé has brought meditation to us in a way that even the 'busiest,' non-foofoo-ist business leader can embrace, nourish, and apply to their lives. Rob brings magic to the idea of 'doing nothing' as being the most in service thing you can do if you are committed to powerful and authentic leadership and impact in the world. I'm personally grateful for this man and what he brings to everyone he touches, and I highly recommend anything Rob offers... And let's start with this book.*"

—ANESE CAVANAUGH, CREATOR OF THE IEP METHOD AND AUTHOR OF *CONTAGIOUS CULTURE*

"*As leaders, we have the honor to develop freedom and responsibility within a culture of discipline. do**nothing** challenges our conventional way of thinking and encourages leaders to take pause on a daily basis—further developing their skill to be truly present and responsible with their teams.*"

—TOM WALTER, CHIEF CULTURE OFFICER AT TASTY CATERING

"Less is more! In a world full of noise, silence is golden. Silence and stillness give you peace, let you deal better with stress, make you more creative and more productive, and reconnect you to yourself and others. 'Be quiet' becomes 'be positively powerful'! That's the paradox of our age: you don't need to do more to become more successful and fulfilled. You need to do less."

—RAUL CANDELORO, BRAZILIAN SALES AND
MARKETING SPECIALIST, AUTHOR, SPEAKER,
COACH, CONSULTANT—STILL WORKING ON
THE "LESS IS MORE" AND "QUIET" THING.

donothing

Breathe in

breathe out . . .

Love + gratitude,

Rob

donothing

The most rewarding leadership challenge
you will ever take

rob dubé

LIONCREST
PUBLISHING

*do**nothing***

The most rewarding leadership challenge you'll ever take

ISBN   978-1-5445-1002-6 *Paperback*

978-1-5445-1003-3 *Ebook*

To the love of my life, Emily, and our children, William and Frances.

I love you more than words can describe.

Contents

· · · · ·

Foreword

By Bo Burlingham

· · · · ·

I knew Rob Dubé as an entrepreneur long before I became aware of his passion for meditation. I had met him in a seminar I was helping to teach at ZingTrain, the education arm of Zingerman's Community of Businesses in Ann Arbor. The seminar was related to a book I had written called *Small Giants: Companies That Choose to Be Great Instead of Big.* After the seminar, I had kept in touch with Rob. He and his business partner, Joel Pearlman, had a company, imageOne, in Oak Park, Michigan, that specialized in managing the printing needs of its corporate clients. From the first, I was struck by their eagerness to adopt the most innovative business practices they could find as well as their commitment to creating in imageOne the kind of company that all of the people in its orbit—employees, customers, suppliers, community members—would love to be associated with.

In 2009, another entrepreneur I knew, Paul Spiegelman, started the Small Giants Community, with my support. Rob soon became one of its mainstays, and our relationship deepened. I discovered that he was a serious meditator when he volunteered to lead meditation sessions at our annual conferences. That was welcome news to me: I had been meditating for more than forty years.

It had actually been my wife, Lisa, who had started me off in the late 1970s by going to the Transcendental Meditation Center in Cambridge, Massachusetts, where we lived, to sign up for a class on meditating. By then, Transcendental Meditation (TM) had already achieved some fame thanks mainly to the Beatles, who had learned to meditate from TM's founder, the Maharishi Mahesh Yogi himself. When Lisa returned from the center, she told me that it was having a two-for-one special. I decided to sign up for a lesson as well, mainly out of curiosity.

I had no idea what to expect, but I did know that, the Beatles notwithstanding, I was not interested in joining any sort of cult. Not that TM is a cult. It most assuredly isn't, but I didn't know much about it at the time, and I didn't want to take a chance that it might be. In fact, I was so cautious that I asked my TM instructor whether it was necessary to accept the Maharishi's teachings to experience whatever it was that meditating provided. She told me, no, I simply had to follow her instructions, and I could have the full meditation experience.

And that's what I did. After receiving my mantra and a brief introduction to the practice, I started meditating for twenty minutes twice a day. I could see the physical benefits almost immediately. At the time, I had a good deal of stress in my life, and it had manifested itself in a variety of ways—a chronically nervous stomach, twitching eyelids, hemorrhoid flare-ups, general edginess. Those symptoms all but disappeared within the first two weeks of meditating. The stress didn't go away, but it didn't have the effect on me that it had had before. I must have acted differently as well, because Lisa could always tell if I had missed one of my sessions. "You didn't meditate, did you?" she would say and then encourage me to take twenty minutes to get back on track. The experience itself I found hard to describe to other people, partly because, as Rob says, it involves doing nothing—and, above all, not thinking. Somehow doing nothing left me feeling calmer, more balanced and centered, and at peace with the world. I enjoyed it and became quite dependent on it.

Finding time to meditate was not a problem for the first few years, as I was writing freelance back then. But after our second child was born, I realized that I had to find a real job. A headhunter, referred by a friend of mine, contacted me in 1981 about a writing position at Fidelity Investments. I assured her I was the wrong candidate—I didn't even know the difference between a stock and a bond. She said Fidelity could teach me all that. The company just wanted a capable writer.

So I went in for an interview and was hired. I hoped to be able to keep meditating but feared it would be frowned upon in a financial firm. I asked my new boss if I could exchange my lunch break, which I didn't need, for about half an hour alone in my office in the late afternoon. "Oh, you're a meditator!" he said. "So am I." It turned out that Fidelity had brought in a TM trainer a few years before, and some employees, including a couple of portfolio managers, had kept up the practice. We put together a small meditation group, and I meditated with my colleagues when they were available. Otherwise I meditated on my own and kept on doing it after I joined *Inc.* magazine a year later.

That was my only experience with businesspeople who meditate, and I didn't think much more about it until Rob told me how important meditation had been to him, as the president of imageOne, to have a regular meditation regime and to go on silent meditation retreats. In talking to him, I quickly realized that he knew a lot more about the subject than I did. I was merely a devoted practitioner.

Rob had studied it, researched it, thought deeply about it, looked into the science behind it, identified business leaders who swore by it, and generally immersed himself in the world of meditation.

I understood his enthusiasm. I had often recommended meditation to friends, especially those prone to anxiety, because I thought they would be happier people if they took it up. Rob went quite a lot further. Like the Maharishi, he thought meditation could change the world—the business world in particular. Among other things, he believed it could make people better leaders, and he made a very persuasive case for that, which you can read in chapter 2.

I realized over time that Rob was serious about rallying other people in business, especially entrepreneurs, to his cause. For openers, he was writing this book, which I gathered would serve as a sort of manifesto for a movement. I have been part of several movements in my lifetime, most recently those associated with Small Giants and open-book management. I'm not sure what this "do nothing" movement will look like, although I suspect it will have something in common with the large Transcendental Meditation community in Fairfield, Iowa, which is not only a beautiful and peaceful place, but also one of the most entrepreneurial towns in the country.

In any case, I'm very happy to join Rob in summoning businesspeople to meditate. They will be better off for it, and so will everyone else in their lives. Meanwhile, I'll keep doing what I've been doing for the last forty years—namely, nothing.

BO BURLINGHAM, EDITOR AT LARGE, *INC.*
MAGAZINE, BESTSELLING AUTHOR OF *SMALL
GIANTS: COMPANIES THAT CHOOSE TO BE GREAT
INSTEAD OF BIG*; WRITER AT LARGE, *FORBES*;
COAUTHOR OF *THE GREAT GAME OF BUSINESS*

Introduction

Why Leaders Should *do**nothing***

· · · · ·

You have a lot of reading choices, and I'm grateful to you for starting by reading these first few words of *do**nothing***. I won't assume you are familiar with all the benefits of a daily meditation practice. Briefly, the meditation being written about in *do**nothing*** is often referred to as "mindfulness meditation," which is simply sitting quietly and paying close attention to your breath.

I'm curious why you're reading this book. Maybe someone you know noticed that you are ready for meditation. Maybe, consciously or unconsciously, you realized on your own that you are ready, and somehow this book landed in your hands and you began reading. Was it the title: *do**nothing***? With the busy lives we lead, doing nothing can sound quite appealing! Was it your search for the next phase of your leadership? Give it some thought: *Why am I reading this book right now? Why did this interest me?* Please pause, think about why, and consider writing down your thoughts.

You're already an excellent leader. You've gotten to where you are today because you care about people—and we all know that when it comes to the successes of our companies, it's all about the people. As a leader, you've likely been consciously or unconsciously on a leadership journey. You've been learning what it takes to be great: working with a mentor or two, attending conferences, reading books, listening to podcasts, taking workshops, participating in businesses groups: the list goes on.

At some point, it's likely you've been exposed to the benefits of a regular meditation practice and considered or even committed to a consistent—or inconsistent—daily practice. You probably know that a regular meditation practice has the power to help you, over time, become more aware and have greater presence. Maybe you've already heard how a regular meditation practice can help to work the compassion and empathy "muscles" in your brain. Later in this book, you'll read about some of the science behind that.

How do you feel when you're with another person and

you're totally connected? I've learned that when I give another person my full attention and presence, things slow down. I think more clearly. My judgments go away. I make better decisions. Most importantly, the person I'm with feels that energy from me. That energy changes their outlook—maybe for the moment, for the day, or for the entire week. This has a direct impact on the work they do, the interactions they have, and their physical and mental well-being. I affect that. When I truly realized that my actions—my presence—could affect a person that deeply on a day-to-day basis, it was humbling.

We've been given this gift: the gift to lead and make a difference in the lives of others. We get to choose how we use that gift. When we are given such a gift in life, aren't we responsible for learning how to utilize it best? I think so, and, as you read this guide, I will share how you can use mindfulness meditation to do just that.

This book will give you insights from leaders who have found the time to start a daily practice, including my own story (it's short!). It will give you an overview of the facts and science from thousands of studies that have shown meditation to be an effective way to shape the brain. The book will also teach you how to meditate—that part is easy!—and what to expect when you make the commitment to start a daily meditation practice.

This is a commitment to improve your mental health. Much like a physical workout routine, I've learned that you must do it regularly and stay disciplined to see results. In *The Book of Joy: Lasting Happiness in a Changing World*, the Dalai Lama and Archbishop Desmond Tutu share how important mindfulness is to your inner peace, likening it to a healthy immune system: "Think about it this way. If your health is strong, when viruses come they will not make you sick. If your overall health is weak, even small viruses will be very dangerous for you. Similarly, if your mental health is sound, then when disturbances come, you will have some distress but quickly recover. If your mental health is not good, then small disturbances, small problems will cause you much pain and suffering."

I've set this book up as a simple and quick guide to learning about the benefits of a daily meditation practice, as well as a how-to guide for getting started, from creating a practice discipline to learning how to sit properly.

All in all, this book is intended to be a quick read to get you comfortable with the simple life tool of meditation. I've found that it has changed my presence in the world and directly benefits those around me as I flow through this life. So, let's start learning about *your* journey to becoming a better leader, spouse, parent, family member, friend, and person in the world.

PART I

Why Meditate: Benefits for Business Leaders

chapter**one**

A Journey to Compassionate Leadership

· · · · ·

From Selling Blow Pops to *Forbes*'s Best Small Giants: The imageOne Story

Like you, I'm on a journey.

When I first started my business in 1991, a meditation practice was the furthest thing from my mind. In fact, it would be more than a decade before I tried it out and discovered how much meditation could benefit my leadership. In hindsight, I've realized that so many aspects of my career and personal journey led me to ultimately uncovering my meditation practice, and I've learned many important lessons in leadership, business, and mindfulness along the way.

My career journey started in 1983, when my best friend, Joel Pearlman, and I started selling Blow Pop lollipops out of our locker as freshmen in high school. Joel's uncle owned a drugstore, and he would sell us Blow Pops by the box for five cents each. We resold them for twenty-five cents each at lunch. The product was so popular that kids were lined up and down the hallway waiting for us to arrive. It was a great product, good profit, and fun!

Many years later, Joel and I reflected on that time in our lives and realized that was when the "entrepreneurial bug" bit us. As we progressed through school, we had all sorts of businesses together: copying popular music onto blank cassette tapes and selling them for half the price as a store-bought tape—which we quickly learned was illegal—selling T-shirts in college, and even a healthy car-detailing business one summer.

Despite all the practice we had starting businesses together, when college graduation rolled around, we still didn't know what we were going to do with our lives. Then Joel came across a small ad in the back of a magazine about an emerging business: replacement toner cartridges for a new technology called laser printers. The concept was to "recycle" the cartridges by taking used, empty ones apart, cleaning them, filling them with new toner, and putting them back together. Joel mentioned it to me, and we both thought it was a cool idea and great way to save customers money on a new technology. Sounded good to us! We followed up, went to Austin, Texas, to learn the process, and the next thing we knew, we were starting our business, imageOne, out of Joel's parents' basement in 1991.

We grew through hard work and a little luck, but mostly through our commitment to providing an extraordinary customer experience. We had to: the cartridges we recycled only worked 50 percent of the time. Unlike Blow Pops—guaranteed to satisfy the customer—this product would likely upset a business's day-to-day activities. We quickly learned that cartridge recycling was not our strength and decided to outsource the production to a professional toner-remanufacturing company. Our business evolved from a toner company to a "managed print services" company, where we managed—sold, serviced, and supplied—the multifunction printers and copiers used in businesses.

We grew from nothing to $6 million in sales over the next thirteen years. For some, that growth is amazing, and for others, it may sound like a snail's pace, which is how we felt—ever striving to be big but not really knowing why. In 2003, we had a breakthrough: a contract at a large hospital, which quickly became a game-changer for us. Throughout the process, there was tough competition for the contract, yet somehow, we were able to win it over a billion-dollar public company. Losing the contract to a much smaller company caught the attention of the executives at the big public company. Midway through 2004, they approached us to ask if we might be interested in selling imageOne to them and staying on to operate it as a wholly owned subsidiary, which would become their Managed Print Services division.

During the period of due diligence on the part of both companies, I became extremely stressed and anxious. Growing up and throughout my adult life, I suffered from constant anxiety, caused in part by my parents' divorce when I was young and then by adolescent OCD (obsessive-compulsive disorder). However, by most measures, I was able to get past the day-to-day crippling feelings and lead a productive life as a husband, father, and entrepreneur.

Now, we were juggling the daily tasks of running the business while going through the process of selling the company in a secretive manner. We were not sharing what was happening with the rest of our team, which was entirely out of alignment with our values. At the same time, we were getting excited. We would have an upfront payout, a three-year employment contract, and an additional payout over the next three years if we hit extremely realistic goals.

It seemed that selling would also bring some additional security and opportunity to our team members. The proposal would keep imageOne as a wholly owned subsidiary, and we would not have to reduce our staff. The public company had five hundred salespeople located throughout the United States whom we would train to sell imageOne's services as a new product line. On the surface, it seemed like this was a no-brainer. It wouldn't take much effort to take imageOne from $6 million to more than $50 million in the next few years. Although selling wasn't something we had ever intended to do, we moved forward, and in December 2004, we officially sold the company.

I remember the day vividly. I was scheduled to be the parent volunteer in my daughter's classroom. In the morning, I went to our attorney's office to sign the paperwork. From there, I headed over to her school. The next thing I knew, I was in a classroom of twenty second-grade kids who didn't know, and more importantly didn't care, that I had officially sold my business. It was surreal: I had expected some sort of fireworks ceremony to take place, but, fittingly, it was the complete opposite. That evening, I met up with Joel for a celebration dinner. We were both exhausted, Joel had a horrible cold, and we weren't in much of a celebratory mood. It seemed like the perfect way to cap it all off: staying grounded and humble.

Then, reality hit. For the first time since college, we were employees. Our new titles? "Vice President of Something or Other"—we don't remember the titles they gave us, and we didn't care. We just wanted to do amazing things. But we weren't accustomed to working at a public company with more than three thousand employees. Suddenly, we had a boss. When we had a vision, we wanted to go make it happen—*now*. The company had amazing people, but we just weren't clicking with the culture. Our values weren't in alignment. There were lots of changes, and they happened regularly. My good friend and mentor, Gino Wickman, who created the Entrepreneurial Operating System (EOS) and authored the best-selling book *Traction*, always told me, "Vision without execution is hallucination." That's exactly what was happening. Over time, Joel and I started to lose the passion and excitement we had when we were first acquired. We started daydreaming together about the end of our contract and starting a new business. We knew we wouldn't stay with the company any longer than we had to.

A year later, my anxiety was at an all-time high. It all came to a head when I was on "vacation" in northern Michigan with my family. It was a beautiful day, the family was out enjoying it, and I was inside the house working. At some point, I paused and felt this overwhelming feeling of helplessness come over me. I'd read about meditation in the past and even researched its benefits and how to do it, but I'd never found the time to try it out. That day would be different. I looked over at a chair in the corner of the room and said to myself, "Go sit in the chair, close your eyes, and focus on your breath for five minutes." I did, and I felt better!

My curiosity about this feeling blossomed, and I continued my journey, first on my own, and then with a local meditation teacher, Donna Rockwell. During my first session with Donna, I told her I wanted to learn how to meditate. She asked me what I knew, and I shared what I'd been doing. She told me it sounded like I already knew how to meditate—that's how *simple* the practice really is—but she'd do a session with me anyway.

We sat in chairs, and she instructed me to sit upright with my hands on my legs, feet firmly on the ground. She said to close my eyes and start focusing on my breath—breathing in, breathing out. When thoughts arise, notice them; say, "Thinking," to yourself; and just return to the breath. *Easy but hard.* At the end of the session, I opened my eyes and said, "How did I do?" Donna laughed and explained that just sitting is an accomplishment. There is no good or bad, right or wrong. The practice of meditation is just that: practicing awareness of your thoughts so you don't react instantly. Viktor Frankl, a Holocaust survivor and the best-selling author of one of my favorite books, *Man's Search for Meaning*, says: "Between stimulus and response lies a space. In that space lie our freedom and power to choose a response. In our response lie our growth and our happiness."

At the beginning of 2006, a new CEO came into the company. Joel and I requested a meeting with him to share the frustrations we were experiencing. That March, we traveled to the company headquarters in Tampa, Florida, to discuss what had been happening over the past fifteen months. Just a month later, the CEO contacted us and shared that Managed Print Services wasn't going to be part of their strategy moving forward. Then he said, "Would you like to have the company back?"

On the surface, it probably seems like we would have jumped at the opportunity, but we both felt we had lost our passion for the industry after this experience. Taking the company back meant we would have to shift our thinking—and fast. I felt a familiar sense of anxiety and stress settling around me, but this time was different. Nine months prior, in August 2005, I had started a regular meditation practice, and it helped me handle these stressful events better than before.

The awareness muscle I was developing allowed me to slow down and start to notice things that were happening in my life in a different way. Small things can make a big impact when they are noticed. For example, in the middle of this big decision, someone happened to send me the book *Small Giants* by Bo Burlingham. To this day, I'm not sure who sent it or why, but whoever you are: *Thank you.* I saw the book's title and tagline: *Small Giants: Companies That Choose to Be Great Instead of Big.*

I opened the book and started flipping through it, noticing a familiar company name, Zingerman's Delicatessen, located in Ann Arbor, Michigan. During college, Joel and I would frequent Zingerman's. It is a small deli that has great food, but, more importantly, an over-the-top customer-service experience. We would order our sandwiches, sit down at a table, and marvel at how they operated the place. Every employee there was energetic, knowledgeable, empathetic, helpful, and had amazing energy. We always said that if we ever started a business together, this is the type of service experience we would have. At imageOne, that is exactly what we did and continue to do to this day.

I immediately read the book's chapter on Zingerman's and learned more about the company than I already knew. Their story of building a values-based business was inspiring. As I kept reading, I learned about companies all over the United States that operated in a similar fashion: Caring about employees in the totality of their lives. Making a difference in the community. Leaders who know who they are and what they want out of business. Amazing company cultures. And strong financial results. These companies often practiced open-book finances, making employees financially literate, so they can make smarter, more informed decisions for the company. After finishing the book, all I could think was, *Wow*. I was inspired and shared the book with Joel. He felt the same way, and we agreed to take imageOne back with a new philosophy in mind, striving to become a "Small Giant." In June 2006, we became owners again, with a renewed sense of purpose for what we were meant to do.

That inspirational deli I mentioned? They've grown well beyond a corner storefront and are now a $60 million community of businesses. One of those businesses is ZingTrain, a company that provides business workshops on everything from customer experience to open-book management to visioning. Joel and I started sending team members to ZingTrain to participate in the customer-experience workshops, and, in 2006, I was invited to participate in their visioning workshop. The workshop is designed to teach the Zingerman's visioning process: a system for creating a sound and inspiring company vision.

I'll be sharing some of the visions I've created with this process later.

While at the workshop and having lunch, I found myself in line next to a particularly inquisitive gentleman. I've found that curious people are rare in the world, and this person was not only inquisitive, but also seemed to know the exact questions to ask about me and my business. After a line of questions, I turned the tables and started asking about him. "What do you do?" I asked. "I'm an author," he said. The book-writing process fascinates me, so this really piqued my interest. He went on to share that, during his career, he had also been the editor at *Inc.*, a publication for growing businesses. This again piqued my interest: while growing up, *Inc.* was my favorite magazine. I continued with my questioning only to find out that the person I was speaking with was Bo Burlingham, the author of the book I'd just read, *Small Giants*.

Over the next day and a half, I shared my story with Bo. We continued our conversation and exchanged contact information before parting ways. Bo and I kept in touch and, a year later, he contacted me with an idea. He wanted to put together a group of eight to twelve entrepreneurs he believed were emerging "Small Giants" and take them around the world to visit more mature "Small Giants" companies. We would meet with founders, executive teams, and employees at two to three companies twice a year in different cities. During these trips, I had the opportunity to meet well-known and not-so-well-known leaders, and I learned from and was inspired by all of them. Like the leaders profiled in Bo's book, their approach to building a values-based company focused around six core qualities:

Purpose: Small Giants have a vision, a powerful mission statement, and core values that can be brought to life.

Leadership: Small Giants are made up of servant leaders who believe in leading with values.

Culture: Small Giants foster a culture of intimacy by putting employees first, caring for them in the totality of their lives.

Finance: Small Giants believe in protecting their gross margins without compromising company values.

Customers: Small Giants cultivate meaningful relationships with customers, suppliers, and all stakeholders.

Community: Small Giants understand the value of establishing deep roots in their community.

As I got to know Bo better, I learned that he and I had something else in common: a daily meditation practice. In fact, it was such an important discipline in his life that, when he didn't meditate, his wife, Lisa, would notice the difference. "If I'm feeling a bit stressed or edgy, Lisa will tell me, 'Bo, you didn't meditate today. Please do us all a favor and do that!'" Some of the most inspirational leaders I know have a daily meditation practice. In a survey conducted by the Institute of Mindful Leadership, 93 percent of leaders reported that meditation training helped them create space for innovation. Seventy percent reported that it helped them think more strategically.

Small Giants leaders know who they are and what they want out of business. As it relates to building a values-based company, a common theme resonated with me: these leaders care about their employees and the totality of their lives. This idea inspired me to bring a more compassionate leadership philosophy to imageOne. I've always cared about people, I've always been clear about what I want out of business, but how could I raise the bar as a leader? What could I do differently that would make my team sit up and take notice?

After a decade of hard work implementing these new ideas, I can humbly share that imageOne was honored as one of twenty-five companies listed as *Forbes*'s Small

Giants: America's Best Small Companies of 2017. As I write this book, we've grown from a $6 million company with twenty team members to more than $15.5 million with sixty team members in twenty-six states. The philosophy of compassionate leadership that my meditation practice helped uncover guided us as we built a values-driven business that puts people before profit. Today, our company values guide the daily behavior of every person in the company, our purpose inspires our work and helps us grow with integrity, and our manifesto shares with the world what we're all about. We keep these pillars visible in our office, we vocalize them at every company-wide meeting, and we incorporate them into every aspect of the business.

imageOne Values:

We have a passion for the extraordinary: Customer, Team, Community

We are open and honest: Integrity, Humility, Vulnerability

We execute flawlessly: Easy, Efficient, Reliable

We think like visionaries: Create, Improve, Solve

imageOne Purpose:

We deliver extraordinary experiences that positively impact the lives of our team members, the goals of our customers, and the fabric of our community.

imageOne Manifesto:

imageOne's business is document lifecycle management. We take care of your entire document environment: from managed print to process automation to document security. Our job is to manage and optimize your environment, anticipate your needs, and help you realize your business goals.

Our process works because each and every team member cares about their role, understands how it impacts results, and works to deliver extraordinary customer experience. In fact, we're obsessed with it.

What's it like to work with us? We're easy, efficient, and reliable, and we're always, *always* improving. Our team is united by an unwavering commitment to client success. We are passionate about what we deliver and how we deliver it, and we're proud to call it the imageOne Way.

imageOne 2026 Vision:

Saturday, April 4, 2026. An unseasonably warm spring day greets all imageOne team members from near and far as they gather at imageOne headquarters for the all-company meeting and celebration of imageOne's thirty-fifth anniversary.

As all iO team members gather in the office, they take a second to appreciate the down-to-earth, warm feel of the space. There is a beautiful café with cozy booths that line large windows, letting in the sunshine and natural light. The booths are comfortable enough to have one-on-one meetings or enjoy lunch with a customer or coworker. Even the remote team gets to enjoy a free weekly coffee on imageOne: a small gesture to show that all team members are appreciated.

All team members also enjoy health benefits, such as gym memberships for remote team members and an on-site facility for local team members, complete with a shower room for those who want to run or bike to work. It is also a place to go for meditation or a spin on the stationary bike. A luxurious rooftop space tops it all off.

Glancing around the new space, there are bold monitors displaying the most up-to-date metrics on the business. There is a sense of pride in the air as the displays read that the team has reached its goal of $60 million in sales. With the company running like a well-oiled machine, those numbers will *continue to grow, prompting team members to start thinking about where they are going to spend their next bonus! imageOne's philosophy of caring for the totality of the lives of our team members has been our marketplace differentiator. Our customer retention remains an astounding 100 percent, and, through our sales and marketing efforts, we are deluged with new business opportunities. With a closing ratio of more than 50 percent, the next ten years are going to be even more exciting than the last.*

Throughout the new space, there are bits of the imageOne brand and how it has become synonymous with our unique culture. From the Extraordinary Customer Experience *book to the customer surveys, testimonials, and referrals that flash on the screens, it is evident that we not only wrote the book on customer experience, but are living it every day. We are deeply ingrained in our communities, making small and large differences in the lives of others.*

Our Innovation Lab is focused on research and development projects and receives feedback and input from people in other roles who have great ideas. This has been critical in uncovering the new, exciting, and profitable products and services that serve our customers' needs in markets we never imagined. Our process—researching, experimenting, and thoughtfully going to market—has allowed us to skyrocket the company's growth and profitability. The result of our formula of delivering extraordinary experiences is that we are positively impacting the lives of our team members, the goals of our customers, and the fabric of our communities.

As everyone gathers into the iO auditorium, local and remote team members alike share stories from recent sabbaticals and engage in friendly banter about life balance. They discuss the most recent training and development sessions that they've attended and talk about the positive energy and latest technology surrounding them at iO HQ. There is an excited buzz in the crowd as they patiently await a celebration that has been ten years in the making. The lights dim, and the entire team breaks into boisterous applause. The imageOne CEO takes the stage.

"Welcome, everyone, to the celebration of imageOne's thirty-fifth anniversary. It is thanks to each and every one of you that we are here today.

"It seems like just yesterday that we were building our ten-year vision, polishing it, and discussing it together as a team..."

It is my goal, in the pages that follow, to help you come to understand the science and methodology of how meditation can help you become a better leader: not 100 percent better but—to build off the title of Dan Harris's book on meditation, *10% Happier*—10 percent better as a leader.

Here's the exciting part: as you stay with it, the benefits compound! The more I practice meditation, the more aware and present I become, and the better I am for and to the people I lead, allowing them to be their best, too.

I've identified four key benefits of my meditation practice, which have taken me to new levels of success as a leader and in business:

1. **Productivity and Efficiency**: As a result of my practice, I have a clear mind on a day-to-day basis that notably increases my productivity and efficiency. When I first started meditating, my mind began to open like it hadn't in years. Now when I meditate, ideas start flowing in, and, although I'm not writing them down, the best ones rise to the top; and, by the end of my session or a retreat, I've had some real breakthroughs. It might be a new product idea, a problem I've been trying to solve, or a solution to a deal I've been trying to close. As I deepened my practice, my productivity and efficiency drastically improved, allowing me to train my attention and give my full, complete presence to the task at hand.

2. **Letting Go of Fear**: Whether I realized it or not, many of the decisions or nondecisions I've made in business have been based in a deep-rooted fear. It could

be a fear of failing or of being outside of my comfort zone. With a regular practice, I've come to realize that nothing matters but this moment. I'm an authentic person and, when vulnerable or feeling that I might fail, I'm better able to put my ego aside and do things that are scary: the types of activities that have brought me greater success. And, even when something does fail, I've learned to reframe the experience and the story in my head. Was it a failure, or have I gained new wisdom? I get to decide.

3. **Mind-and-Body Rejuvenation:** When I'm on "vacation," it feels busy. I'm often on the go with lots to do and see. Even if I'm lying on a beach, I'm not just lying there; I'm usually reading and learning. An active mind. A mind that is somewhere other than where I really am. I might be learning about new marketing techniques instead of taking in the fullness of the beauty of Lake Michigan, the feeling of the sand on my toes, and the sounds of children playing. During my daily practice, I've learned to build the skill that allows me to be more present wherever I am at any given moment. Meditation also allows time for my mind and body to rest and rejuvenate. I'm a physically active person with an extremely active mind. I've noticed that, at times, this can get overwhelming. My practice allows me to notice what I didn't before.

4. **Perspective**: My practice brings unsolicited perspective. I've got the stories of the day, week, month, and my life playing in my head constantly. Time to quiet my mind brings me back to now: what really matters. What if these were my last breaths during this lifetime? Would I be happy with the way it was ending? Was I caught up in a story about something that happened at work, the slow line at the store, or something one of my kids said to me? The perspective that my practice has brought me is that most of these things really don't matter at a deeper level. It's love, kindness, and compassion that matter. Time and again, my practice brings that perspective back to me.

chapter**two**

The Case for Meditation

· · · · ·

Have you ever been meeting with a team member and begun thinking about an email you just read, a client you need to get back to, your child's grades, or maybe your plans for the weekend? I know I have. That person I'm with, the person sitting across from me, is another...*person...a human*. I know, I know, that's obvious. But why isn't it obvious to us, as leaders, that we need to give the person across from us our full, focused attention? The type of attention I might give when a doctor is giving me a diagnosis, or my child is telling me about an accomplishment.

I believe that my presence as a leader makes all the difference in the experience of team members—the people who work at imageOne—at my company. It doesn't mean we'll always agree on everything. In fact, my presence may help both the team member and me realize that we weren't meant to work together—that there is a lack of alignment. Conversely, by slowing down and becoming completely present, I start to see qualities in team members that I hadn't noticed before. I become part of the "lifting up" rather than "holding back" process.

What do I mean by "lifting up" and "holding back"? Let's start with "holding back." In most cases, my team members are only going to be as good as I am until they change their position in the company and have interactions with other high-level leaders, or leave. I've found this is a responsibility most leaders believe they take seriously, but really don't. I know, because I had to challenge myself to do better, too. It begins with our own growth, both personally and professionally. Sure, we might take seminars on leadership and management. We might watch TED talks and read articles on the latest and greatest ways to motivate our teams. We attend conferences to hone in on our industry craft and network with leaders in similar roles.

These are all important growth tools, but there's a tool that is much more powerful and transcends the rest: learning to be truly aware and present. For me, that means: Getting the ongoing chatter in my head to subside. Being able to put away all distractions easily and quickly so I can listen to my team members with a clear mind, instead of making deductions or assumptions while listening. Not solving—in my head—while listening. Pausing, which can feel uncomfortable sometimes, has actually become a great way to allow what I've heard to "settle" for a minute before I respond.

Words matter. My presence and energy matter. Remember, *"Between stimulus and response lies a space. In that space lie our freedom and power to choose a response. In our response lie our growth and our happiness."*

When team members know I've given my full energy and presence to them, they will appreciate the outcome of the conversation, even if it doesn't go exactly as they would have liked. When I am not growing my "awareness" muscle, I am holding back my team members' growth. They are people, just like me. They are looking to me and how I conduct myself in business as a template for how they will lead and manage people in their careers and lives. As Ellie Burrows, cofounder of MNDFL meditation, puts it: "There is no greater honor than supporting someone's growth and evolution as a human being."

By "lifting up," we become highly aware. When I am "lifting up" team members, I notice their strengths and weaknesses at a whole new level. I am more patient with their "weaknesses" and begin creating thoughtful plans to maximize their strengths and help, where necessary, improve any perceived shortcomings. I better understand what's important to my team members and why, which allows me to gain greater insight into enhancing their life experience with the company. By "lifting up," we become an active part of team members' life journeys, helping them become their best selves.

While growing up, and even now as an adult, one of the most important things to me was to have my parents' attention. They didn't need to agree with me, spoil me, or coddle me. They just needed to be there, not only physically but mentally. When that happens in life, it's magical. There is an energy you feel from the person you are with, whether it's a parent, spouse, child, or just the person sitting next to you on a plane. You can feel when you have the full attention of another human being, and that feeling provides fulfillment. It's not about hearing what you want to hear: it's about being heard.

We all face problems and distractions that cause us great stress. Former Vice President Al Gore certainly did. In *The Book of Joy: Lasting Happiness in a Changing World*, the Dalai Lama shares a conversation the two of them had, in which he urged Gore to stay mindful and keep perspective. "I said to him that we human beings have the ability to make a distinction between the rational level and the emotional level. At the rational level, we accept that this is a serious problem that we have to deal with, but at the deeper, emotional level, we are able to keep calm. Like the ocean has many waves on the surface, but deep down it is quite calm."

Are you a great leader? Do you have room for improvement? Even if you answered that you're not yet great, but you are a pretty darn good leader—and you must be if you're reading this book—you have some level of humility. As a humble person and leader, you likely also have a level of self-awareness, and you want to continue to learn and grow. How great of a leader do you want to be? Are you willing to take extraordinary steps to get there? Take a minute and think about amazing leaders. What were they willing to do to become the best? Pete Carroll, head coach of the NFL's Seattle Seahawks and a daily meditator, says, "The best have a commitment to excellence and growing, getting out of their comfort zone." Are you truly the *best*? Are you willing to get out of your comfort zone?

Through a regular practice of meditation, you will begin to listen, really listen, in a whole new way. Not listening and thinking at the same time, which is critically different. Meditation trains you to be focused on *now*. This moment. Most of us are consistently focused on the past and the future, all while knowing that there is nothing we can do to change the past. And although we like to think we can control future outcomes, the fact is that we cannot. We can only set ourselves up for a desired outcome. So, the present moment is all we have. Jon Kabat-Zinn, founder of the Mindfulness-Based Stress Reduction program at the University of Massachusetts, says, "If you want fear, get a future, and if you want to be depressed, get a past!"

Tim Ferriss, successful entrepreneur, best-selling author of *The 4-Hour Workweek*, *Tools of Titans*, *Tribe of Mentors*, and many other books, and host of *The Tim Ferriss Show* podcast, reminds us that you will begin to bring your meditation practice, cultivated over time, into real-life scenarios where you would normally "react." Instead, you're likely to pause and be thoughtful about your response or action. For Ferriss, there's a big payoff: "When I meditate consistently, my reward is getting 30 percent to 50 percent more done in a day with 50 percent less stress. Because I've done a warmup in recovering from distraction."

More than ever before, mindfulness is being used across disciplines to effect positive change. Many schools are implementing mindfulness programs as an alternative to traditional disciplinary actions. A 2014 study published in *The Journal of Child and Family Studies* followed the behavior of 409 San Francisco Bay Area elementary schoolers, before and after meditation intervention. These mindfulness practices resulted in seven weeks of improved behavior. In late 2016, a *U.S. News & World Report* article reported on meditation practice at Robert W. Coleman Elementary School in Baltimore, Maryland, where traditional detention has been replaced by a Mindful Moment Room. When students misbehave, they spend time in the room, practicing deep-breathing exercises and talking through what happened. Research shows that the program is working: for the past two years, the school has reported zero suspensions.

The University of Wisconsin's Center for Healthy Minds often uses an MRI (magnetic resonance imaging) machine in its research. Studying the effects of meditation on the brain structure of both beginning and experienced meditators, they have found positive physiological effects. One of their best-known studies was with Matthieu Ricard, a Buddhist monk and experienced meditator. Over the course of twelve years, he was regularly asked to meditate while in an MRI machine, hooked up to more than 250 sensors. The changes that took place in his brain were overwhelmingly positive compared to that of a non-meditator. In fact, the scan showed that his brain was producing a groundbreaking level of the gamma waves linked to consciousness, attention, learning, and memory. After the results of the study were released, Matthieu's

TED talk "The Habit of Happiness" was viewed almost seven million times. Media coverage around him and the study's findings surged, with publications such as *Business Insider*, *GQ*, and *Time* declaring him to be the "Happiest Man on Earth."

Meditation in Business

There's a compelling pattern developing among business leaders who achieve extraordinary success: they practice meditation. From Steve Jobs to Ray Dalio, these influential leaders have used meditation to increase innovation, harness their energy, and channel their drive into the things that matter most. In fact, their visibility helped in part to inspire my own practice. The various viewpoints of highly successful leaders who meditate allowed me to feel more comfortable that meditation is a life tool that would benefit not just me, but those around me, in large ways and small.

Most leaders find that when they commit to a regular meditation practice, their work and their lives greatly improve, and they gain a competitive edge in their business, leading them to new heights of success. Likewise, my practice has contributed to my own business successes. I never imagined that I would be able to share that *Forbes* Magazine ranked my company as one of *Forbes*'s Top 25

Small Giants: America's Best Small Companies of 2017.
Many factors played into this honor, but I know my meditation practice helped me be a better leader.

As I delved deeper into my meditation practice, I was surprised to find many major conferences around the United States focused on neuroscience, meditation, and mindfulness. In 2008, I attended one of those conferences, Wisdom 2.0, on a whim. The conference focuses on mindfulness in life and business, and I've attended every year since. Many of the speakers come from technology companies on the West Coast, such as Google, Facebook, Twitter, LinkedIn, and Salesforce.com. I learned that not only did leaders in these organizations meditate, but the companies had all created internal programs to encourage meditation among employees.

But, at the end of the day, we are in business, so what does all this mean for our companies and bottom lines? Why are these leaders implementing meditation programs at their companies? Let's look at a few case studies of the positive effects of meditation on business, starting with my own company, imageOne.

imageOne: Business Decisions, Team Members, and Partners

· · · · ·

Whoops, I Messed Up: How Meditation Could've Prevented a Big Mistake

Part of my role at my company, imageOne, is to serve on a team that manages a few of our larger customers. In early 2005, before I started my meditation practice, I made a mistake I'll never forget. I received a phone call from one of our top salespeople telling me she had just been informed that our largest account, the Borders bookstore chain, was leaving us to work with a new vendor.

Reflecting on that moment now, I remember that my first reaction was anger. I was angry at our salesperson for not being more on top of the account. Angry at the customer for not being respectful enough to give us a chance to retain their business. Then I felt fear. What would this mean to the business and to me? Yes, what *would* it mean to me? Anger and fear. Two emotions that would not serve me well in this situation. I was angry, I was fearful, but there were two things I was not: aware or present.

As I went into fear mode, I decided to use a network I belong to in order to go higher up in the Borders' organization to tell the tale of how we were treated during the process. I placed an inquiry through my network and quickly received a message from the administrative assistant of someone who was friends with the CEO! I was excited and called back right away. The assistant told me that, although her boss was out of town, she also knew the CEO and would be happy to place an inquiry with him about sharing my story. She asked me to email her the details, and she would put me in touch. But that isn't what happened. She did forward my email on to the CEO's assistant, who then forwarded it to a good number of people within the company, including our main contact. Within hours, we received a call from our contact, letting us know that nothing would change except one thing: I had burned a bridge.

As painful as the story is to tell—even though I tell it all the time—it's a great reminder to myself of how unaware I was during that time of my life, allowing my emotions to rule me and acting without thinking. Ultimately, my lack of awareness led to irresponsibly putting the company in a difficult situation: not only did we lose the client, but, despite all the good things we had done for them when they were our customer, we would certainly never receive a referral.

I can't blame them for that. I can only blame myself. As the Dalai Lama explains in *The Book of Joy: Lasting Happiness in a Changing World*, fear and anger are naturally connected, and the two emotions destroy a calm mind: "Anger is no use in solving problems. It will not help. It creates more problems. Then eventually through training of our mind—and using reasoning—we can transform our emotions."

I believe if I had had a regular meditation practice in place back then, I would have been able to assess the situation with awareness, slow down, and better understand where the customer was coming from. I would've been able to look within and ask myself the question: "Why was it so easy for them to stop doing business with us?" Now, with a regular meditation practice in place, I am grateful to them for the lessons they taught me, and I'm confident—well, fairly confident—it's a mistake I will not make again.

Recently, I put what I learned from that experience and my meditation practice to the test. Our relationship with a large customer—I'll call them F100 for the purposes of this story—has been the opposite of what we had with Borders. It's a true partnership where we believe in helping each other succeed. We started out slowly, handling some small sites for F100 and proving ourselves to be worthy of handling their entire enterprise. F100 is a large company, and things don't always move fast: people are often promoted or change roles, and a number of people participate in making decisions.

My company's business is document lifecycle management, which means we manage everything from printers, including multifunction printers (MFPs), to digital documents within an organization. Printing is expensive, and it's our goal to help companies reduce their print costs through digital processes and end-user education. Until recently, the "bread and butter" of our business and our main source of profit was print management. Helping companies reduce print is what we do best, and that means consistently helping our current customers reevaluate what they're doing. If we do our job right, we help them spend less money with us! We love helping people and know that, if we do the right thing, great things will result.

F100 was the beneficiary of our passion for helping, and,

over several years, we were able to help them cut their spending with us by almost half. While this was the right thing to do, it did bring up a challenge for us. Because their annual spend with us was significant, they were receiving extremely advantageous pricing. As their spend went down, we were finding ourselves close to a break-even point. With a contract in place, it seemed there wasn't a whole lot that we could do, short of dropping them as a customer, which was really never an option! Halfway into 2014, we realized the effect F100's reduced spend was having on our business: we weren't hitting our numbers, and it didn't seem as though we would. Instead of having an emotional reaction, however, I stayed aware, present, and level-headed.

First, I shared what was going on with the rest of the company. I then decided to meet with our main contact at F100 to discuss our situation. My meditation practice has helped me be more vulnerable, and our F100 contact was receptive to what I shared with him. This began a two-and-a-half-year process of putting a new contract in place.

In retrospect, those two-and-a-half years were rewarding. But there were many times when I wasn't sure we were going to be able to keep the contract secure, since part of their process required them to speak with other companies to ensure that they were still getting a fair deal. We had to work with many people within their organization to educate them about our situation. At various points during the process, I would receive urgent requests for different types of reports and data, and I found myself creating a story in my head about why those requests were being made. The longer the process became, the bigger the story got: Could they be strategizing to leave us and stalling until they had everything set up for a smooth transition?

My many years of meditation practice helped tremendously during this time. I was consistently clear-headed *most* of the time. I could recognize that I was creating worst-case-scenario stories in my head that were making me anxious. When people in my company were feeling anxious as well, I was able to lay out the situation clearly and simply, and stay confident that it would work out the way it needed to. What that meant I wasn't sure, but I knew I needed to let go, which doesn't mean I didn't show up. There is a difference. Letting go means accepting that, despite your best efforts to control things, whatever happens is part of your journey. You can't get too attached to outcomes. The key is to consistently *show up* and do your best work. That's all we can control.

In this case, the outcome was positive. We agreed on new contract terms that allowed us to continue to help F100 reduce their print costs, while keeping our gross margins in line. Throughout the process, what I went through mentally, though not easy, was ultimately rewarding. There is a saying: "Stressed? Meditate. Not stressed? Meditate more." I love this, because it reminds us that working out our awareness and presence muscles puts us in a position to be better prepared for the uncertainties that inevitably come our way in business and in life.

Meditation, Leadership, and Dealing with Challenges

My company, imageOne, had a tough year in 2014. We were coming off a couple of strong years and feeling confident until midway through 2014, when we realized we were not going to hit our budgeted sales or profit numbers. In fact, it was possible that, for the first time in our history, we might be operating at a loss. The executive team was concerned, rightfully so, and a few "panic meetings" took place.

These meetings stick out in my memory because I distinctly remember feeling very calm and clear about what we needed to do to get things back on track. I intuitively knew that it was part of our journey as a company, and that good things were going to happen as a result. No, I'm not psychic. I was simply tapping into my awareness and drawing on experience and wisdom, as well as the knowledge that we had a healthy balance sheet and could withstand this bump in the road.

My meditation practice was extremely helpful during this time. Not in the way you might think: the main benefit wasn't because I was coming home at the end of a long day and meditating to calm my nerves and anxiety, although that was certainly helpful. It was that all the time I had spent practicing meditation prior to this difficult moment really paid off. Remember: "Stressed? Meditate. Not stressed? Meditate more!" It's like practicing free throws or three-pointers in basketball, shooting over and over again. When the game is on the line, all that practice allows you to sink the free throw or hit that three-pointer to win the game before time expires.

Speaking of games: it was that same clarity and uncanny confidence that allowed me to make one of the best decisions I've ever made as a leader, which was to teach and implement open-book finances using the philosophies from Jack Stack's excellent book *The Great Game of Business*. Through my involvement in the Small Giants Community and my friendship with Bo Burlingham, I had met Jack many times. I would regularly share with him that, although I thought his Great Game of Business system was great in theory, it wasn't great for my company for many unique reasons. Jack would smile and chuckle at me, as if to say, "Oh, your company is so different from all the rest?" He'd heard that excuse a million times in the past.

With the company at a crossroads, I finally began the vulnerable journey of rolling out the Great Game of Business program at imageOne. Why vulnerable? Although I'd been reading our income statement and balance sheets for years, I never had to teach or explain them to anyone else. Facing a year that was looking to be break-even or possibly a loss, the information I would be sharing with my team was not going to be pretty. In fact, to some, it could be a cause for concern. My years of meditation practice allowed me to approach this in a calm and patient way.

Quickly but thoughtfully, I began to outline the program, educate our team members, create a bonus program, and implement "mini-games": ways to save money or increase productivity. We began to develop a monthly rhythm of sharing our income statements and balance sheets at every "all-hands" company meeting. The results surprised me! We quickly found areas in which to save and ways to be more productive. That first year, we went from a break-even, possibly losing scenario to a profit. In the years since implementing the Great Game of Business, our profits have risen to an all-time high, with 2016 and 2017 being our best years in business.

Also from a team-member perspective, 2014 was a challenging year. Once again, I relied on my meditation practice during the difficult decision to change the role and lower the compensation of a longtime, highly valued team member whom I'll call Lisa. As much as we wanted to keep Lisa's role and compensation in place, one of the many reasons we were struggling was that she was in a position that didn't suit her. She wasn't motivated to grow within that role and was significantly overpaid, earning around $150,000 annually. To complicate things, Lisa had a busy household with three children and was her family's main source of income. I knew her husband, and, like Lisa, he was a wonderful person. This further complicated what I knew I had to do.

After giving a great deal of thought to the matter, I decided to ask Lisa to meet me at a local trailhead for a hike. During our walk, I explained our situation to her, what had to happen, and that, at this point, it wasn't negotiable. I was focused, direct, and clear with her, and, although it was apparent she was unhappy with my message at the time, I learned two years later that Lisa appreciated my approach with her on that day.

In hindsight, she realized this was the push she needed to reevaluate if this was really what she wanted to do with her life, and, if so, what she needed to do to succeed in her role. For me, the experience was humbling. It was one of the most difficult team-member conversations I've ever had, as I knew it would affect not only Lisa's ego but, more importantly, her family finances. I pledged to support her no matter what, whether she decided to leave the company or recommit to her role and get back to her current level within imageOne. I'm proud to say that Lisa stayed with the company and has been working hard to climb the ranks. At the beginning of 2017, she was brought back into a senior position.

Taking a mindful approach to our communication and Lisa's situation made a huge difference. Lisa appreciated my honesty, humility, vulnerability, and authenticity, and I credit my regular daily meditation practice with putting me in the right mindset to allow things to unfold that way. Our team members deserve our full presence, consideration, and compassion, and when we give it to them, it pays big dividends.

Business, Friendship, and Meditation: My Partnership with Joel Pearlman

When I was in fifth grade, I met my best friend—my brother from another mother—Joel Pearlman. Between fifth and eighth grade, we were on-again, off-again friends. Today, I still tease him about not inviting me to his Bar

Mitzvah. Of course, I'm over it now. It's all a part of my meditation practice!

In ninth grade, with our friendship growing closer, Joel and I decided to embark on what would become our first entrepreneurial venture: selling Blow Pop lollipops out of our shared locker at school. As I've said, this is when the entrepreneurial bug really bit us. After experimenting with several smaller businesses throughout high school and college, we started imageOne together in 1991. Joel and I have been working together through thick and thin ever since.

The successes and challenges of running our company, imageOne, have been ongoing since day one. We both have strong personalities and opinions. We are master debaters, and we are both usually right. There have been times in our partnership where both of us have had enough of the other, wanting to leave and do something different on our own. After all, wouldn't that be easier?

Prior to my regular meditation practice, our partnership was at times a source of anger, anxiety, and frustration. Joel and I are both fairly self-aware: we work on ourselves; we work with therapists and with business and life coaches; and we regularly meet off-site to discuss our lives. At the end of the day, we both agree that our friendship is of top importance. As many others have told us, a business partnership can be like a marriage. It takes effort. Even with that awareness, partnerships still cause angst! I've spent many nights wide awake, running through a conversation we had earlier in the day and sometimes finding myself arguing with Joel in my head.

In the thirteen years since starting my meditation practice, I've noticed a huge shift in our partnership. I'm more aware during conversations and in meetings, and able not to go into "debate" mode. I'm more patient—usually—and able to listen fully before thinking of a response, judging, or reacting quickly. I'm more aware of how Joel might be feeling on any given day: maybe he didn't sleep well the night before or has other things on his mind. Most importantly, I've learned to truly accept Joel for who he is, not what I want him to be. Although we think and do things differently, he has incredible talents that I don't possess, and, as a result, we really complement each other. I attribute this awareness to my meditation practice.

In 2016, we created our 2026 Vision for imageOne, which I included in the first chapter. This was a collaborative process, and, when it was done, it became a source of inspiration for the entire company. As part of the vision, we know we will need to move our offices to a larger space. With all the new and amazing energy happening in downtown Detroit, a group of us got excited about the prospect of moving there. When we rolled out the final vision to the entire team, we used pictures to illustrate the many inspiring things that 2026 would bring, including a picture of a building that appeared to be in downtown Detroit.

Joel and I regularly hold off-site "same page" meetings, where we discuss issues, challenges, opportunities, and how to support each other's life goals. I mentioned that I was excited about moving downtown and would love to try to make that happen as soon as possible. To my surprise, Joel was confused. He was open to the idea, but ultimately preferred our offices to be closer to his home, ideally in the downtown of one of Detroit's thriving suburban cities.

My immediate reaction was shock and disappointment, but my meditation practice allowed for me to recognize my feelings at that moment, instead of reacting strongly. I was able to share my feelings in a healthy way, try to understand Joel's perspective without comparing it to my own, and move on. Joel and I had a healthy discussion and decided to talk with our team to hear their thoughts on moving to downtown Detroit versus the downtown of a local suburb. My frustration didn't go away immediately, but the discipline of my ongoing practice prepared me for these types of discussions.

Ultimately, we agreed to be open to both scenarios and to making a solid, collaborative business decision, which may mean moving to downtown Detroit or someplace else. At the moment, it's looking as though we will open a satellite office downtown as a first step, to test the waters and see whether our team likes it.

At our Annual Planning Session (APS) in January 2017, I had another opportunity to use skills cultivated in my meditation practice. The APS consists of two days dedicated to planning for the upcoming year. The session was flowing well, our executive team was well prepared, we knew what we needed to do, and we were focused. The financial and tactical goals we set were challenging but realistic. We were feeling great.

Toward the end of day two, it was apparent we would be finishing a bit early. Since we had some time, Joel asked if we could address a couple of other issues unrelated to the APS. Conversation ensued and turned contentious. Joel and I were going into "debate mode," and I was feeling attacked at times. Joel's energy on the topic was strong, and after two days of strategic discussion, I didn't have the energy to meet him where he was. Suddenly, I noticed myself becoming highly aware. My mind quieted, and I let go. We completed the discussion as a team and brought the meeting to an end.

When we end meetings, each participant answers the following questions: What is your feedback from the meeting? Were your expectations met? Where would you rank the meeting, from 1 (the worst) to 10 (the best)? The feedback was overwhelmingly positive, but when it came to me, I ranked the meeting a 7.5, because Joel and I had put the team through our "debate." I was physically and mentally drained. Once everyone left the conference room and I was organizing notes, Joel came back in, unresolved. We started discussing the issue again, and our talk ultimately got heated. Again, I noticed what was happening and was able to quiet my mind as Joel vented his frustrations. At one point he said, "You're just sitting there acting like you're listening, not saying anything, and it's really pissing me off!"

Before my meditation practice, I would have snapped back. This time, I was highly aware. I simply told him that it was true, I was *trying* to listen, but that it was hard to do given the frustration, tension, and energy between us at that moment. But I was trying, and that was the best I could do right now. The conversation didn't end on that day. We chose instead to give it some time and allow our thoughts and feelings to settle. Big surprise: the next time we spoke about it, we had a healthy and much more productive conversation.

chapter**four**

The Science of Meditation

· · · · ·

Before moving on to more examples of the value of meditation in business, let's look at four different scientific studies of meditation's benefits. The first two focus on meditation's social and cognitive effects; the third and fourth deal with the physiological changes that meditation can bring about. These are only the tip of the iceberg of the research that's been done on meditation, which you'll learn more about later.

Contemplating Mindfulness at Work: An Integrative Review

This study, whose primary investigator was Darren Good of the Pepperdine University School of Business, was published in the *Journal of Management* in November

2015. It describes what mindfulness is, gathers facts from more than four thousand scholarly articles on the topic, and addresses its surging presence in organizations such as Google, Aetna, the Mayo Clinic, and the US Army. At the time of publication, 13 percent of US workers reported engaging in mindfulness-enhancing practices.

Mindfulness is "receptive attention to and awareness of present events and experiences." Although this is said to be the common understanding of mindfulness, the researchers felt it was too ambiguous to help understand how mindfulness intersects with workplace functioning.

The review showed that mindfulness affects human function through attention, which alters other domains of basic functioning. Mindfulness has been shown to improve three qualities specifically associated with attention: stability, control, and efficiency.

Why is this important? The human mind is estimated to wander roughly half of our waking hours. *Half!* Mindfulness has been shown to stabilize our attention in the present moment. Imagine bringing just one-third or two-thirds of those wandering moments back to the present. How much better would you be as a leader? Imagine how efficient you would be. Could you do eight hours' worth of work in four hours' time? What could you do with an extra four hours a day?

The review showed that those taking mindfulness training, ranging from just a few to thousands of hours, reduced mind-wandering. Those same individuals were shown to be able remain vigilant longer while performing both visual and audio tasks. The more experienced meditators showed reduced activation in the neural network—indicative of wandering mind and mind chatter—and brain patterns consistent with sustained attention. The study theorized that attention stability is likely a result of the meditators actually noticing their minds wandering and, through the practice of meditation, now being able to bring their minds back to the present moment.

Pioneer psychologist William James still said it best in his classic *Principles of Psychology,* first published in 1890: "The faculty of bringing back a wandering attention over and over again is the very root of judgment, character, and will."

The World's First Study of a Multisession Mindful Leader Program

Studies from a Harvard University Mindful Leader program, published in the *Harvard Business Review* in

November 2016 with the title "Mindfulness Works but Only If You Work at It," involved fifty-seven senior business leaders in two different training groups. Both groups learned about the benefits of mindfulness and how it might impact their leadership. They also learned how to practice and apply mindfulness to leadership challenges. The participants were assigned a "buddy," another leader in the program, and given home mindfulness meditation practices for every day of the course. The Harvard researchers' goal was to understand if and how the practice might be helping the leaders with real work issues.

The results were not surprising. It was found that simply attending one or more workshops may help strengthen resilience by sharing useful tools and techniques. However, other improvements require practice, and the more practice, the better the results. In the study, the leaders who practiced for at least ten minutes each day progressed significantly more than those who did not.

The Harvard study identified three leadership capacities that mindfulness practice develops:

- **Metacognition:** This is the ability, at crucial times, to choose simply to observe what you are thinking, feeling, and sensing. It is like stepping out of a fast-flowing and sometimes turbulent stream onto a riverbank, so you can actually see what's going on. When you learn to do this, you can better see your thoughts, feelings, sensations, and impulses for what they are. Without metacognition, there is no way of escaping automatic pilot.

- **Allowing:** This refers to the ability to let what is the case, be the case. It's about meeting your experience with a spirit of openness and kindness to yourself and others. It's not about being passive or weak, but simply owning up to what is really going on in each passing moment. Without allowing, our criticism of ourselves and others crushes our ability to observe what is actually happening.
- **Curiosity:** This means taking a lively interest in what shows up in our inner and outer worlds. Without curiosity, we have no impetus for bringing our awareness into the present moment and keeping it there.

One leader from the study summed up by saying, "I now have moments of choice that I didn't have before." The study went on to report: "This is because these three qualities opened up a space in the leaders' minds helping them to become less reactive and more responsive, affecting other skills such as regulating their emotions, empathizing, focusing on the issues at hand, adapting to situations, and taking broader perspectives into account."

Psychologist Ron Siegel and the Science of Mindfulness

In a 2015 talk at Google, Harvard Medical School psychology professor Ron Siegel addressed recent studies that demonstrate how mindfulness practices can be effective tools to help resolve anxiety, depression, addictive habits, stress-related medical disorders, and even pain.

Physical pain and discomfort are things many of us live with on a day-to-day basis. Whether it's as simple as the common cold or as complicated as a chronic back condition, pain is involved. When we are in pain, it makes it difficult to be at our best. Our minds aren't quite as sharp. We don't have the same pep in our step. Often, we react poorly, because the pain causes us to have a bit of a short mental and emotional fuse. As leaders, this is not the impression we want to give our team members. We want to lift them up, not drag them down. When we're in pain, it takes a stronger meditation practice and awareness to do this.

In his talk, Siegel discussed a recent study on pain, where participants were divided into two groups: people with a regular meditation practice and those without. The participants were placed in an MRI machine, a cylinder-shaped device that leaves just a person's feet hanging out the end. While in the MRI machine, the participants had their brains studied while various amounts of pain were administered to their feet to cause discomfort. The study found that the regular meditators found the pain less unpleasant and could observe it less reactively. Open monitoring—awareness of our thoughts and feelings, observing them without attachment—reduces the unpleasantness and suffering associated with pain, because you are focused on one thing: the sense perception of that which is around you. Those with a regular meditation practice were also found to have less anxiety during the time leading up to the induced pain.

During this study, two things were happening in the brain from a neurobiological perspective. The insula is a part of the brain linked to emotion and bodily functions, such as perception, motor control, and self-awareness or noticing sensations in the body. Studies have shown that, over time, this part of the brain gets larger in those with a regular meditation practice.

The prefrontal cortex is responsible for evaluating and regulating emotional responses. When regular meditators were exposed to pain, they had decreased activity in the lateral prefrontal cortex, which is responsible for evaluating pain sensation, and increased activation in the posterior prefrontal cortex, which registers sensation. When this happens, a person feels pleasure and pain more vividly but gets less upset by and reactive to them. They are able just to "be" with what is happening.

Mindfulness Increases Regional Brain Gray-Matter Density

In a study that appeared in a 2011 issue of *Psychiatry Research: Neuroimaging*, a team of Harvard researchers at Massachusetts General Hospital found that participating in an eight-week mindfulness meditation program positively impacts the brain. This study, which involved MRI, found that mindfulness practice leads to increases in regional brain gray-matter density. Researchers obtained MRI images of the structures of sixteen participants' brains for two weeks before and after they took part in an eight-week Mindfulness-Based Stress Reduction (MBSR) program at the University of Massachusetts Center for Mindfulness.

During the program, the participants held weekly meetings to practice mindfulness meditation: focusing on the nonjudgmental awareness of sensations, feelings, and states of mind. They were also given audio recordings for guided meditation practice and asked to keep track of how often they practiced each day. During this same period, sets of MRI brain images were taken of a control group of nonmeditators.

The meditation group spent on average twenty-seven minutes each day practicing mindfulness exercises. They were given a mindfulness questionnaire that indicated significant improvements compared with preparticipation responses. The MRI images showed increased gray-matter density in the hippocampus, an area of the brain known to be important for learning and memory, and in structures associated with self-awareness, compassion, and introspection.

The MRI images also showed decreased gray-matter density in the amygdala, which is known to play an important role in anxiety and stress. No change was seen in the insula, a structure associated with self-awareness, despite earlier studies that had shown some change. The researchers determined that longer-term meditation practice would likely be needed to produce changes in that area of the brain.

None of these changes were found in the control group of nonmeditators. This led the researchers to conclude that the structural changes in the brains of those in the meditation group had not resulted merely from the passage of time. This important study helps further prove that mindfulness practice produces positive effects on psychological well-being by impacting emotional regulation, memory, learning, and perspective.

chapter**five**

Meditation and Corporations: Aetna and CEO Mark Bertolini

• • • • •

My company, imageOne, is a "Small Giant." I've found that meditation helps me considerably in my role there. But what about larger corporations: "big giants"? Let's look first at Aetna, one of the biggest health insurance companies in the world, and its CEO, Mark Bertolini, and then follow up with a glimpse at the tech behemoth Google.

CEO Mark Bertolini is passionate about the way we lead. Mark, who was named to *Fortune*'s Top 50 list of the World's Greatest Leaders in 2015, has been CEO of the diversified healthcare benefits company since 2010.

Mark grew up in Detroit, where he attended Wayne State University, before earning his MBA from Cornell University and held executive positions at Cigna, New York Life, and SelectCare.

In 2001, Mark received some news that would change his life. His then-sixteen-year-old son was diagnosed with a rare form of cancer. Mark immediately dedicated his full time and energy to his son's treatment. For the next three years, Mark devoted himself to his family until his son's recovery in 2003.

Then, just afterward, in 2004, Mark himself suffered a severe skiing accident in Vermont. He was headed down a run, glanced back to check on his kids, and ran into a tree. The accident caused him to lose consciousness for a week. He woke up to find himself with a neck broken in five places, a broken back, and a partially paralyzed left arm. In fact, he learned that he had almost lost his life: the crash landed him into a freezing river, causing hypothermia, which prevented the life-threatening spinal injury from killing him. As Mark recovered, doctors gave him the traditional medications for managing pain: a mishmash of strong doses of painkillers, none of which were helping physically or mentally.

At this point, Mark was introduced to his now-life partner,

Mari, a specialist in cranial-sacral therapy, a gentle, non-invasive form of bodywork that addresses the bones of the head, spinal column, and sacrum. Its purpose is to release compression in those areas, which in turn alleviates stress and pain. With a curiosity and openness to alternatives, Mark tried it and, to his surprise, was off his medications within three months. This was the beginning of the journey that led him to yoga and meditation as another way to help strengthen his body and cope with the pain from the accident. Prior to the accident, Mark would run four miles a day and loved the endorphin rush this gave him. Mari suggested he try yoga, and, as a yoga teacher and practitioner herself, volunteered to teach him.

Before they started, Mari practiced yoga on her own using just one arm, so she could relate to and teach Mark the best poses for his body. He began his yoga practice and, to this day, every morning at 5:30 a.m., he does thirty to sixty minutes of viniyoga, a style of yoga focused on adapting to the individual's unique condition and needs. After his yoga routine, Mark sits in meditation for fifteen minutes to an hour each day, depending on what his schedule will allow. Although now known to many Westerners as a type of workout that can get extremely intense, yoga is actually a practice to train our bodies to sit in meditation for long periods of time.

As both Mark and his son were healing, Aetna, knowing

Mark's successful turnaround background, called him for help. Although he didn't have the time to take on a fully dedicated role, he did some work for the company as head of special products to help get it on the right track. In 2010, with his son's health improved and a little nudging from Aetna, Mark assumed the role of company CEO.

When Mark became CEO, Aetna's stock price was thirty dollars per share. As he traveled around the country to meet with the many amazing people who made up the company, his awareness and presence were high. He began to hear what he refers to as "whispers," subtle and not-so-subtle comments and clues from company employees that they were struggling, unhappy, and having trouble making ends meet. His practice allowed him to pick up on this message and act.

Mark shares that he might have approached things differently prior to his practice, removing himself from the struggling employees' emotions. Not that he didn't care, but he had a job to do and couldn't solve everyone's problems. Now, with a renewed outlook on business and life, Mark made groundbreaking decisions that, at the time, looked risky and, to some, even a little crazy.

Mark decided to look at the employees of the company, invest in them, and create a culture of caring for the totality of their lives. A shift started at Aetna, one that included strong empathy and compassion: action based on doing good and doing well. This was a huge insight for Mark, and the results were amazing.

Mark slowly instituted a series of changes, including voluntarily increasing the minimum wage and reimbursing student loans up to $2,000 per year.

A third of the company's employees have taken a health-and-wellness program that includes education on meditation, yoga, sleep, diet, and nutrition. A new online resource (http://aetna.tumblr.com/mindfulness) was created for employees to access wellness information and encourage moments of mindfulness during the day.

Mark was adamant that data be collected on the meditation-oriented employee health-and-wellness program to ensure that the science behind, not just the feelings about, the results were understood. As of June 2016, more than one-quarter of the company's fifty thousand employees participated in the class. Among that group,

- Healthcare costs were reduced by 7 percent.
- Stress levels were reduced by 28 percent.
- Sleep quality improved by 20 percent.
- Physical pain was reduced by 19 percent.

Employees became more effective on the job, gaining an average of sixty-two minutes in productivity each per week. Aetna estimates this is worth $3,000 per employee annually. Do the math on that! $3,000 multiplied by 12,500 participants equals $37,500,000. Per year! How's that for affecting the bottom line?

Mark noticed, most importantly, that people were just "working with each other better on a day-to-day basis." Demand for the class is rising, and every class is over-booked. He is such a believer that, in 2017, Aetna invested $1 million in the program to build even stronger offerings and deepen research. Aetna also launched a public web-site where you can learn more about their program and meditation: http://aetna.tumblr.com.

In 2016, Mark was the first CEO of a public company to create a role for a Chief Mindfulness Officer tasked with spreading the health-and-wellness message throughout the entire organization. At the end of November 2017, Aetna's stock price had risen—from $30 when Mark took over as CEO in 2010—to $174 per share.

Other CEOs are catching on. Mark's been contacted by Fortune 100 CEOs asking about the programs he has spearheaded at Aetna. His bold decisions have become game-changing, culture-shifting, bottom-line-improving programs that drove the company's stock to all-time highs. A group of these Fortune 100 CEOs, including Mark, participate in the Higher Ambition Group, an organization to help share best practices and spread the word to other leaders. What originally started with five CEOs quickly grew to fifteen: 15 percent of the CEOs running companies in the Fortune 100!

What about entrepreneurs and leaders who aren't Fortune 100 CEOs? What can you do? Mark's advice is no different for you than it is for them: take action. Start where you can, take it one step at a time, and build on those successes. His personal advice? Start a meditation practice. Work on you. During an interview, Mark was asked, "With all you have to do, how do you have time for all of this personal work?" Mark responded, "If I don't take care of myself, then I can't do any of the other things well!" He puts it another way: "I don't believe that anyone can lead effectively unless they have a personal practice that allows them to be their best self every day."

The science on meditation and its ability to enhance your awareness is endless. The evidence is overwhelming. If you are serious about becoming the best leader you can be, a daily practice will move you in this direction, just as it did for many of today's greatest business leaders, including Mark.

chapter**six**

Google Searches Inside Itself

· · · · ·

In 2007, Chade-Meng Tan, a Google engineer who was their 107th employee, and whose current title is "Jolly Good Fellow," had a dream to change the world by utilizing meditation as a tool for a more mindful society. Fortunately, Google was open to the idea, and Tan had the opportunity to create a program within the organization called Search Inside Yourself, promoting mindfulness through meditation. It became the company's most popular training program!

The class focuses on three steps: attention training, self-knowledge/self-mastery, and the creation of successful mental habits. To date, thousands of Google employees have taken the seven-week class, and there is almost always a waiting list when it is offered. In anonymous surveys, participants ranked the class 4.75 out of 5. Tan says, "Awareness is spread almost entirely by word-of-mouth by alumni, and that alone already created more demand than we can currently serve."

Those who have taken the class share that they're surprised by a regular meditation practice's ease and accessibility. One participant said that it is "sort of an organizational WD-40, a necessary lubricant between driven, ambitious employees and Google's demanding corporate culture. Helping employees handle stress and diffuse emotion helps everyone work more effectively." Another participant spoke about the small attitudinal changes taking place among coworkers, which make a big difference. Even learning to be more mindful with email responses has become a benefit!

As word spread, other companies became interested in the program and how they could replicate what Tan was doing at Google. This strong interest led to the establishment of the Search Inside Yourself (SIY) Leadership Institute in 2012. It has since become globally recognized and works with corporate, nonprofit, and government organizations all around the world. To date, more than twenty thousand people in more than one hundred cities have taken the SIY program.

The program has had some remarkable results. When

the Institute measured capabilities before and after the program, here's what they found:

- **Leadership**: SIY participants were better able to maintain calm and poise during challenges. Results: 17 percent preprogram; 46 percent postprogram.
- **Performance**: SIY participants reported a greater ability to focus and be more effective. Results: 36 percent preprogram; 68 percent postprogram.
- **Stress**: SIY participants reported less emotional drain after the program. Results: 58 percent preprogram; 28 percent postprogram.

More Key Takeaways from Search Inside Yourself Research

- Throughout ten years of research, the connection between mindfulness and well-being has been consistent. One study found that two weeks of mindfulness training increased well-being, decreased emotional exhaustion at work, and even increased job satisfaction.
- Meditation has been found to increase brain-cortex thickness and activation in regions associated with emotional awareness and emotion management.
- Training in emotional intelligence (EI) and compassion has shown to reduce interpersonal stress and improve relationships.

- Greater EI has been correlated with higher leadership performance.
- In a survey conducted by the Institute of Mindful Leadership:
    ◦ 93 percent of leaders reported that meditation training helped them create space for innovation.
    ◦ 70 percent reported that it helped them to think more strategically.

chapter**seven**

The Meditative Warrior

· · · · ·

Business people who feel that mindfulness meditation is "soft" and ineffective should meet professors Holly Richardson and Matt Jarman, who teach classes on meditation at Virginia Military Institute (VMI). Holly also teaches physical education and Matt teaches psychology, and they've both incorporated meditation concepts into their coursework. On a recent episode of the ABC News podcast 10% *Happier,* hosted by Dan Harris, Matt and Holly shared their experiences implementing these new methods at VMI.

Matt is a psychologist with a background in meditation, a practice he started in graduate school while working on his PhD. He read about the positive effects of meditation, especially on stress levels. Ultimately, he started his meditation practice not only to decrease the stress he was feeling, but also to become more efficient and increase his ability to concentrate. For Matt, it was and still is all about being more mentally efficient. He meditates daily because he knows he won't be nearly as productive if he doesn't: he becomes more scattered. His practice is a 15-minute meditation each morning and, if he's feeling depleted at the end of the day, another 15-minute session before getting back to work with renewed energy.

Holly learned the Mindfulness Based Stress Reduction (MBSR) meditation technique created by Jon Kabat-Zinn, PhD, Executive Director of the Center for Mindfulness at the University of Massachusetts Medical School. After reading his book *Full Catastrophe Living*, she began the daily practice of meditating on the breath that I'll share later in this book.

Holly is passionate about teaching meditation to cadets for two reasons. First, she feels that, personally, she loses her cool more often when she doesn't practice, and that when she does practice, she feels like a more authentic person. Second, she cites the many studies that show how helpful the practice can be to military men and women who return from stressful combat situations with Post-Traumatic Stress Disorder (PTSD). Matt and Holly have found that mindfulness is equally helpful in reducing the likelihood of PTSD in those who have yet to be deployed.

With respect to the very serious matter of PTSD, cadets are aware of how many soldiers return from combat with post-traumatic stress and want to avoid this if they can. Meditation practice allows those with PTSD to see the signs and symptoms coming on and use their practice to become present, still, and aware. Even a small thing such as focusing on the breath can change an individual's mindset. It helps soldiers create the ability to switch from the traumatic memories playing in their head back to the present moment, reminding them of where they are right here, right now, safe and okay. The practice helps service members be more relaxed and less reactive to emotions, dampening high-highs and low-lows, cultivating an even keel. Meditation trains those yet to be deployed for both when they are in combat and when they return. Research has shown that the practice teaches cadets skills that reduce postcombat stress, so they are less likely to come back home with PTSD.

Reactions from the cadets taking the class have been open and positive. Holly believes the science behind meditation is a key component, but there's also the environment the cadets are in: they have extremely structured and stressful days from the moment they wake until the moment they go to sleep. As a result, they are open to trying different techniques that will help them better manage their experience.

Matt's class at VMI is a leadership course called Modern Warriorship, a requirement for all cadets. He chose the name to combat any stereotypes of meditation that students may have, because he truly believes that to be the best leader—or "warrior"—they can, meditation is a helpful, even necessary, process.

In his research, Matt has studied change using cognitive and social processes. A warrior is literally "one who creates change," the root of the word being "war": creating disorder to change an undesirable situation. This, of course, includes change that will benefit others, which is the goal Matt and his students strive for. To be exact, warriorship is the mental and physical training that allows for you to be more effective in creating positive change. It's about being ready when the opportunity arrives, whether big or small, and in any environment—from a conflict in war to just helping someone on the street. If you're better prepared, you can make better decisions, resulting in fewer casualties, both in war and everyday life, including business.

The biggest challenge for the cadets is no different than for you or me: starting and keeping the meditation practice. When setting cadets up for a successful practice, the focus is on individuals and their environment. The class also focuses on the science showing that you will not lose time by meditating, as you might believe at first, but gain time through increased productivity and efficiency.

Some cadets express concern about how they might be perceived by other people, such as a roommate, who might see them as weak for meditating. Matt explains that true leadership sometimes involves going against the grain. The "Warrior Spirit" involves stopping and taking stock of what is going on, versus allowing the momentum of daily life to take over. He relates how meditation is similar to taking medicine: if the doctor says a medication will help you heal in a healthier and faster way, you've got to take it every day for it to be effective. The same applies with the discipline of a daily meditation practice.

By the end of the course, Holly and Matt have proven to the cadets that meditation is not a soft thing. It helps them lean into and face their fears and stresses head on. They're leaning into them. The lesson is clear: to be your best, to be able to help others effectively, you first need to be able to help yourself.

chapter**eight**

Marathons, Meditation, and Commitment

· · · · ·

Many business leaders draw inspiration from the similarities between running a company and sports. Cultivating excellence and a competitive spirit are common threads in both. When I was young, I struggled with several health issues, including asthma, eczema, and a serious allergy to peanuts. Getting and staying healthy through athletic activity, such as running, has been an important part of my life.

For many runners, and certainly for me, the discipline is about more than just physical fitness. Running is often a mental escape, providing temporary distraction from our day-to-day lives. I started running before I started my meditation practice, and, when I brought the two habits together, the results made a big difference in both my physical and mental health.

I had always dreamed of being able to run a full marathon but never actually believed I could...until I was inspired by Karla Stickney, a team member at my company. One day, Karla shared with me that she was training to run the Detroit Marathon with her then-boyfriend, now-husband Pete. I was inspired and spent the next six months doing marathon training. When Karla and Pete signed up to run the Bayshore Marathon in Traverse City, Michigan, I decided to make that my first attempt.

We got together and decided to give the race added purpose by raising money for autism, a cause near to our hearts. Joel, my business partner and best friend, has a daughter with autism. Danielle is autistic, nonverbal, and an example of mindfulness for all of us, constantly teaching us the power of awareness, presence, and nonjudgment. She's a gift in all our lives and the lives of those around her. Karla, Pete, and I were energized by the deeper purpose behind our upcoming marathon.

The Bayshore Marathon was an amazing experience. I walked for a period and finished in just under four hours. At times, the pain I experienced made me wonder why

I was doing this. Would I finish?! Did I even want to finish? Despite that, I met amazing people during the race. Toward the end, I came upon a man—let's call him Tom—who was walking extremely slowly and looked ready to give up. I encouraged him to run with me, and he did for a bit. As we struck up a brief friendship, he told me he was running the race to show his daughter what was possible. He so badly wanted her to be proud of him—and I am certain that she is!

During the conversation, I got extremely emotional. I finished the race, hugged my family, and shared the stories of people I met along the way. When I started speaking about Tom, I couldn't contain my tears. They were flowing uncontrollably. I knew I had played a small part in helping Tom finish the race and realize his goal of showing his daughter what is possible in life. At that moment, I felt so aware of the interconnectedness we all have with one another, and how we can positively affect each other's lives. After all, I could have just run by Tom and focused on finishing the race myself.

What's this got to do with meditation?

The last week or weeks leading up to the race can become an anxious time for many, and usually did for me. The last seven to ten days of training are known as a "taper" period, where you lower the number of miles you run per day or week and start allowing your body to prepare for the upcoming 26.2-mile run you will take on race day. This taper period may seem like a nice break from daily and weekly high-mileage runs, but my body—and others', I've been told—have gotten used to the longer runs, and, in an odd way, start to crave the running. This causes a certain underlying irritation and anxiousness that can cause people, include myself, to become easily agitated and have a bit of a "short fuse."

While running marathons, I found my meditation practice helpful in making me more aware of the anxiety leading up to the day of the race, which allowed me to be a better person to my family, coworkers, friends, and the world in general. The same dynamic takes place postrace, since after the "high" of the race wears off—for me, within a few days—I would be left with a void while my body recovered. *When can I really start running again—not just short runs to stay loose? And what's next? Another marathon? Am I really up for another three to four months of training and all that goes into running yet another one?*

Since that first marathon, I went on to run thirteen more. All fourteen marathons had the same familiar components of time, training, travel, work/family balance, and the actual race itself. This presented a consistent physical and mental challenge. My meditation practice was instrumental, giving me the mental tools to never get too overwhelmed and to handle all the mental and physical pain I was enduring. For the most part—every step I took toward my goal of completing the upcoming race was a literal step: one aware and present step at a time.

While running a marathon, I experience many different sensations: physical: how my body is feeling; mental: what's going on in my head; the sounds; my fellow runners; the sky and pavement; and, of course, the amazing spectators and the energy they send the runners. Experiencing all that at once can be overwhelming. My practice allowed for me to take it all in, be present, and appreciate the moment for how special it is. Even when tragedy happens.

chapter**nine**

Meditation and Crisis: The Boston Marathon Bombing

· · · · ·

All leaders need to be able to deal with a business crisis, just as we all need to be able to deal with the inevitable crises that occur in our lives. Meditation is a means of dealing more effectively with even the most difficult and extreme situations.

In 2013, I participated in the Boston Marathon. For those who are not aware of its significance, there are a few things to realize about the Boston Marathon. It's the most historic and sought-after race to run. For most marathons, a runner can simply sign up, pay the registration fee, and show up on the day of the race. To participate in the Boston Marathon, runners must qualify by running a different marathon within one year prior and finishing in a time that, based on the runner's age range, qualifies them to run Boston. (An exception is made for a certain number of charity runners who have committed to raising a set amount of money for sanctioned charities.) The race begins in Hopkinton, Massachusetts, a city 26.2 miles from the finish line on Boylston Street in downtown Boston.

The 2013 Boston Marathon was my second time running that race and my thirteenth marathon. As the day unfolded, it would become the most memorable.

When I woke up that morning I was full of the typical mixture of jitters and excitement I get every time I run a marathon. Most runners take a bus to the starting line in Hopkinton. While on the bus, I received a text message from my father, who was in town to support and see me run a marathon for the first time, saying that my grandmother—we call her Memere—had become ill the previous evening and had been admitted to the hospital. His text went on to tell me she was doing well, and I should still run the race. He looked forward to seeing me later, on Boylston Street in front of the Mandarin Hotel, as I approached the finish line.

I had a funny feeling as our bus approached the parking lot of Hopkinton High School, where, each year, a "village" is set up for runners to hang out and prepare for the half-mile walk from the village to the start line. I felt like my Memere was okay, but also that something wasn't quite right. Confused, but highly aware of my confusion, I took this feeling with me as we entered the start corrals. Once in my designated corral, I decided I was going to be laser-focused on the finish line, knowing I would see my family that much sooner and could find out more about what was going on with my Memere.

That's exactly what I did. I ran one of the most "aware" of all my marathons. I was disciplined with my energy, knowing just the right times to expend it and when to hold it back. As I made the left turn onto Boylston Street, drawing closer to the finish, I was most excited to have virtually my entire family within eyesight. This was the first time they had all been able to attend one of my marathons. As planned, they were right in front of the Mandarin Hotel, and I heard my father's distinct, deep voice shouting, "Rob! Rob! Rob!"

Even though it was a thrill to see them, I decided not to stop as I often would in past marathons, for high fives, hugs, and kisses. I felt a strong need to get back to the hotel room. I completed the race around 1:30 p.m. and quickly made my way through the finish area, where the wonderful volunteers give runners food, drinks, heat-sheets—lightweight, aluminum blankets that help keep you warm—your medal, and, of course, your photo. Normally I take my time doing all this, but that day I was on a mission. I quickly moved through, found the bus that held my personal items, then exited the blocked-off runners' area to make my way to where my family and I were to meet.

I actually arrived before my family! These included my wife of twenty-five years, Emily, who flows through life with ease, could teach a class on listening, and supports me unconditionally; my two caring, smart, and independent children, Will and Frances; my brother, Drew, who is twenty years younger than I am, and inspires and teaches me every day; my father, Bob; mother, Carol; stepfather—another Bob—and Uncle Roland. Only my sister, Michelle, a woman who would do anything to help anyone, hadn't been able to travel to the event.

Once they arrived, after a quick exchange of hugs and congratulations, I looked my father straight in the eyes and asked, "How's Memere?" He shared that she was doing great. I was relieved but continued to feel we needed to get to our rooms at the hotel, the Westin Copley Place, which was only a few blocks away. I led the way, walking with purpose and speed. I remember my family saying, "Rob, you just ran a marathon! How and *why* are you walking so fast?" I said that I wasn't sure, I just had a feeling and wanted to get to the rooms. And that we did...

I showered and ordered some food, and we all started to settle in, talking about the day from their perspectives and mine. While catching up, we would look out the windows of our connected rooms, which had a direct view of the finish area, watching the runners come in. Suddenly, at 2:49 p.m., we heard the loudest noise imaginable. The building shook. From the windows, we saw a huge amount of smoke in the air and people running for what looked like their lives.

Unfortunately, they were. We were utterly confused, and everyone in the room was trying to figure out exactly what was going on. There was so much energy in our two rooms—primarily panic and fear. My son, William, who was eighteen at the time, immediately went on Twitter and, holding back tears of fear, told us a bomb had gone off. While this was going on, I somehow remained calm and asked everyone to do their best to do the same. I wanted the group to try to be patient and not attempt to figure out what had happened prematurely. I was aware that social media could be a wonderful resource for communication but could also be filled with rumors. It had been less than a minute since the explosion, and we couldn't panic.

Seconds later, another explosion took place. Something

obviously was very wrong. The room was filled with nerves and anxiety. I motioned to my wife, Emily, to come with me to the other room. We calmly discussed our options and decided that we would leave the city as soon as possible, changing our flight to depart from Providence, Rhode Island, the next day, instead of taking our previously scheduled flight, which left Boston two days later. I called the valet stand to make sure we could leave the hotel and was informed that, yes, we could. I called the airline to change our flight. We began to pack so we could all leave the city together. Since some of my family lives outside Providence, we knew we could stay with them if a hotel wasn't available.

After about thirty minutes, we were ready to go, and I called the valet to have our car brought out. I was informed that the entire city had since been placed on lockdown, and no one would be able to enter or exit. In fact, the hotel had become command central for law enforcement, as they worked to track down those responsible for the bombings. We could not leave the hotel until further notice. Again, I remained calm and rolled with it—which to this day, I attribute to my meditation practice. I quickly accepted our situation, and shortly afterward, I had a thought: considering all the other people stuck in the hotel, we better order some food for dinner now, or else we might be in for quite a wait! I gathered everyone's orders and called room service. I felt great compassion for those who had to work through this, so I placed our order with no expectations as to when it might arrive. Ultimately, we ordered room service four times throughout our stay, and the last time they gave it to us for free because it was fifteen minutes late—a gesture that was totally unnecessary and that I appreciate to this day.

The rest of the afternoon was filled with all sorts of emotions for us. Name the emotion, it was present. During this time, I was aware of those emotions and able to remain level-headed. I thought a lot about my Memere and how she might have directly, through her energy, or indirectly affected me that day, as I ran with extreme purpose toward the finish line. Later in the day, we found out that the second bomb had blown out the front windows of the Mandarin Hotel on Boylston Street, exactly where my family was standing just a couple of hours before. Hearing this only added to what we were feeling. I did my best to understand and be aware and present for everyone. Understandably, emotions were running high. But when I found myself feeling agitated, I used my meditation practice to bring myself back to a loving and understanding place.

Before going to sleep that night, I made meditation a priority. I knew that my discipline up to this point was what had served me so well on this difficult day. Looking out at the finishing area that evening was sad. I remember seeing the siren lights of law-enforcement vehicles still flashing and realizing how serious the situation really was. We didn't sleep much that night, and, in the morning, we were informed that we could leave the city. We would be able to make our flight and get home safely after all.

That first night back home, together at the dinner table, was surreal. The previous day we were in Boston amid such tragedy and sadness, and now we were having dinner at our home outside Detroit, as if we had never been there. But, as I've come to realize with the recent release of an HBO documentary and a major film about the Boston bombings, the memory remains fresh in all our minds.

The Boston Marathon was supposed to be my last marathon for the time being, possibly forever. Later that year, I received a letter from the New York Marathon informing me that my lottery number had been chosen, and I had a spot in the November race. I didn't know what to do. Wouldn't it be dangerous? What better venue for another terrorist attack than forty thousand runners in New York City? Of less importance, but still a consideration, was that I'd have to get back to training, and I had been looking forward to taking a break.

My meditation practice once again helped me through the decision. After thinking deeply about and talking through it with my wife, we decided it would be best to run it and have New York be my final marathon...at least for a while. We felt it was important to face any fears that may have arisen from Boston and to take a stand against terrorists. We would not allow them to affect our life decisions or make us live in fear. In November 2013, I completed the New York Marathon. It was one of my best times and most fulfilling marathon experiences. Looking back on the whole experience, I credit my meditation practice and the discipline I had prior to these events as the "code" that allowed me to handle these deeply chaotic, emotional circumstances with a clear mind.

PART II

Building a Meditation Practice

chapter**ten**

How Do I Meditate? Setting Yourself Up for Success

· · · · ·

As I said earlier, meditating is easy, but hard! Start by setting yourself up for daily success with the right environment and by learning how to sit most effectively.

If you can set up your meditation space to be a regular place to retreat to, that is fantastic. Personally, I set up my home office space, which is quite small, as my meditation space.

The first few times, I would nervously go into my office, shut the door, and start meditating without letting my wife and kids know. They were already somewhat accustomed to respecting my privacy when my door was shut, because it generally meant I was working and not to be bothered. That said, it didn't stop them from occasionally knocking on the door to ask a quick question or share some news.

During those first few attempts to meditate in my office, each time I heard a noise, no matter how slight, I would start thinking my wife or one of my kids were about to knock. *What should I say? Do I get up, turn all the lights on, and act like I was working? Do I have them come in and see me sitting, meditating in the dark? Do I ignore them?*

Okay, okay, back to the breath...

I quickly learned that none of this was worth it. I talked to my wife and shared my intentions to go into my office each night and meditate—and to my surprise, she thought it was a great idea. Then I told my kids, who were twelve and eight at the time. They had a few questions but understood that, when the door was closed, they shouldn't knock unless it was an emergency. All in all, the chatter in my head over this was bigger than it needed to be. And it's wonderful to have support for your practice from those who are closest to you.

From then on, in the evening around bedtime, my kids would say, "Are you going to meditate now?" Thirteen years later, they still know the routine, and it's understood that even if we are traveling, I will be meditating—often in the same hotel room, while they are on the bed with one of their devices or watching TV. (In that case, I wear a pair of noise-canceling headphones!) In my experience, sharing your routine with your family and coworkers is the simplest way to avoid distraction and ensure that you can follow through on your intentions.

In an ideal world, you'd have the "perfect" environment set up in your home: a quiet and serene setting with no distractions to help set the stage for the perfect meditation! Well, I don't know about you, but I live in the real world, and most of us just don't have that.

If you can find a quiet place in your home or your office, let those around you know you'll be meditating for twenty minutes—or however long you choose—so they won't interrupt you. If you have a door to your "quiet" place, close it and turn the lighting down or off.

As you become a more practiced meditator, you'll be able to meditate anywhere—on a plane, on a train, at work, and at home. Quiet or loud: it really doesn't matter where you are. In fact, I've learned to meditate anywhere because quiet isn't the norm: noise is just life around us.

How to Sit

It's a funny question when you really contemplate it: How do I "sit"? As it relates to your meditation practice, comfort is the most important focus. Sitting on a cushion with my legs crossed in front of me is what I prefer, because I enjoy the feeling of being grounded to the earth. Since an important aspect of "sitting" is being upright and aware, I find it most comfortable to sit on my bottom on a cushion, so that I have to do the work of keeping myself upright. I sit on a "zafu"—*za* is Japanese for "sitting"—a circular meditation cushion that you place on top of a rectangular mat, called a "zabuton," which is also cushioned. (You can purchase these in many places; I purchased mine online at www.samadhicushions.com.)

If sitting cross-legged on the floor isn't comfortable for you, try other variations like using a kneeling bench, sitting in a chair, or even lying flat on your back. A kneeling or "seiza" bench allows you to sit with your knees on the floor and your bottom supported by the bench. They are easily available online. If you choose to sit in a chair, as many people do, be sure to sit upright and keep your back slightly away from the back of the chair, supporting yourself upright. It's important that you support yourself, as the idea isn't to be in a total state of relaxation.

However, as I said earlier, being easy on yourself and

ensuring your comfort are the most important points. If supporting yourself in one of these positions takes away from the concentration of your practice, feel free to sit back and be supported by your chair. You can even lie down. Of course, if you lie down, you run the risk of falling asleep, but, as one of my teachers taught me, "That just means you're tired and your body is saying, 'I need some sleep.'" If that's the case, sleep! If you notice your practice regularly becoming nap time, you may want to work on a less supported version of "sitting," such as sitting upright in a chair or sitting on a mat.

I'm in a Comfortable Position—Now What?

It's important to be aware of your posture and its importance during your sitting. The better your posture, the more comfortable you will be, and the more comfortable you are, the longer you will be able to sit without discomfort being a distraction. Like many things in life, when you focus on proper technique—like how a quarterback sets up to throw a pass or a sprinter positions for a race—you maximize your performance. That's why I'm focusing on posture before getting into meditation technique itself.

The approach I have adopted is "The Seven Points of Posture," as taught by Reggie Ray, a Buddhist academic and meditation teacher. Here's a summary.

The Seven Points of Posture

Begin seated in an upright position. If you're on a cushion, your legs are crossed on the mat. If you're on a bench, your knees are bent on the mat. If you're on a chair, move your back slightly away from the back of the chair.

1. Feel your bottom on the seat, grounding you with the earth.

2. If you're on a mat, feel the sensation of your legs crossed on the mat.
   a. If you're on a bench, feel your knees, shins, and feet on the mat.
   b. If you're seated in a chair, feel your legs on the chair and feet on the floor, solid and grounded to the earth.

3. Place your hands with palms down on your legs gently and comfortably. Feel the sensation of the hands touching your legs.

4. Sit with an upright posture: not too rigid, not too soft.

5. Move your chin down slightly toward your chest.

6. Move your gaze slightly downward. If you prefer your eyes open, have a "fuzzy" gaze. If you are sensitive to

stimulation, gaze downward slightly and close your eyes.

7. Move your eyes toward the back of your head, as if you are looking behind you without moving your head—an odd sensation and feeling at first!

A guided audio of Reggie Ray's instructions on posture can be found on Sounds True: http://www.soundstrue.com/store/the-seven-points-of-posture-1989.html. I highly recommend that you download the app and the instruction. It costs $4.99 and is very much worth it.

Instructions for Meditation on the Breath

Now begin to look inside yourself and follow your breath: in through your nose, down through your midsection to the point where the breath stops for you, then back up through the midsection and out your nose.

Follow this last step for the duration of your practice. You will inevitably begin having all sorts of thoughts. This is normal and will be normal for as long as you practice meditation. Very few people, if any, are able to meditate with a completely clear mind. The practice is *noticing*: noticing your thoughts as they arise and simply returning to your breath. In and out, through the nose, the midsection, then back up and out through the nose. Follow the breath until you realize you are thinking. Breathe in, breathe out. Then simply begin again by bringing your focus gently back to the breath.

The practice is working the "awareness" muscle in your brain. This is the value of your meditation and will serve you well as a leader and in your life. Remember the quote by Viktor Frankl I shared earlier in the book: *"Between stimulus and response lies a space. In that space lie our freedom and power to choose a response. In our response lie our growth and our happiness."*

Just like going to the gym for your daily workout, your meditation practice is a daily workout for your mind's awareness and presence muscles. The more you "work out," the stronger they get, allowing you to stop reacting and instead become present, without judgment and chatter constantly running through your mind.

Through your daily meditation practice, you can transform the course of your normal life, positively affecting the way you lead your team and interact with family, friends, and others every single day.

chapter**eleven**

Serious Business Leaders, Serious Meditators

. . . . .

I've found the following two stories of businesspeople who have greatly benefitted from meditation both inspiring and instructive, and I hope you will, too.

Patricia Karpas, Cofounder of Meditation Studio App

Patricia Karpas, referred to in *Forbes* as one of the ten world-renowned meditation tech experts, is the cofounder of Meditation Studio App and host of the popular podcast *Untangle*. In 2016, Apple's app store ranked Meditation Studio as one of the top-ten apps of the year, and *Time* ranked it as one of the year's top-fifty apps. Patricia's professional background includes executive positions at Time Warner, AOL, and NBC, where she was a senior media executive in their New York offices. Prior to starting Meditation Studio App, Patricia was senior vice president of strategic partnerships at Gaiam Inc., a health-and-wellness lifestyle brand.

As the founder of an app focused on helping people start and cultivate their meditation practice, it's no surprise that Patricia has a daily practice of her own. She's been a meditator for more than twenty years, dating back to her days in the corporate world with NBC. After a tough breakup with a boyfriend, Patricia decided to go to an introduction-to-meditation workshop at the Omega Institute. She loved it, and it was enough to pique her interest for further exploration, ultimately leading her to begin a daily practice.

Corporate life can be tough, and back in the early nineties, people were not talking about meditation, especially during her time in New York as a corporate media executive. Patricia kept her practice under the radar, but began to see differences in how she was able to handle work challenges—in a good way. She began to feel that her daily practice was giving her the space to feel more centered and grounded. Her awareness and curiosity started to strengthen. This helped her as an executive, giving her more confidence to collaborate with others—and to understand that she didn't always have to have *the* answer.

During 2015 and 2016, while at Gaiam, Patricia was excited to be part of the team designated to create a meditation app to further promote wellness. Many people within the organization were part of this team, including then-chief operating officer Cyd Crouse, who is now Patricia's business partner and the cofounder of Meditation Studio. Patricia and Cyd, both savvy meditators, had a clear vision for the app's functionality, look, and feel. They also knew that they would need to be mindful of other team members, many of whom had their own visions, which proved to be frustrating at times.

During difficult and passionate conversations, Patricia applied an approach she learned from her regular meditation practice: before responding, stop, breathe, fully listen, and decide, "In the big picture, does this decision really matter?" With that philosophy in mind, she could dedicate her energy to the decisions that *really* mattered while creating an amazing product. It paid off! Meditation Studio has become a success story in the now-crowded world of meditation apps.

As 2016 unfolded, Gaiam was purchased by a private equity firm, Sequential Brands, for $146 million. This transition gave Patricia and Cyd a unique opportunity to take over ownership of the app. Now they could drive their own vision and follow their passion for sharing Meditation Studio app with the world.

As is often the case in business, the initial transition was not without its challenges. Patricia and Cyd, friends and coworkers, were now embarking on a brand-new business partnership. After Cyd negotiated the buyout of Meditation Studio from the private equity firm, the two had to work out ownership and partnership agreements. Working with or for someone is much different than being their business partner. Decisions had to be made on equity breakdown, how much personal money each partner would put into funding day-to-day operations, a buy-sell agreement, and so on. This was an especially difficult time for Cyd, as she was focused on her family as they coped with some serious health issues, and grieving the untimely deaths of her mother and father-in-law.

Patricia's meditation practice was very helpful during this overall stressful time. It helped her to remember to breathe, pause, fully listen, and decide which decisions were truly important. In this case, being mindful took on a deeper meaning, and Patricia was able to empathize with Cyd personally and to approach their partnership agreement in a caring, mutually beneficial way.

Meditation Studio App is a start-up success story partially due to the partners' creative decision to work with some of the best and brightest freelancers. That said, working with independent, talented people can be both a gift and a challenge. Patricia credits her long-term meditation practice with helping her to see and treat these freelancer relationships as true partnerships. She realized that by giving them space to be creative and to be true to themselves, it resulted in a better product and end-user experience. The freelancers may not have always completed projects exactly as she would have done, but she found the end results often exceeded her expectations. She learned that giving up control is sometimes the best solution when dealing with talented people.

During times of frustration, such as when a fee negotiation got contentious, she could let go. As a savvy business person, Patricia knows it's important to get the right result at the right price. Her practice gave her the awareness, during difficult negotiations, to go back to the question she always asks herself, "In the big picture, does this decision really matter?" By helping to cultivate more passion and creativity, the freelancers were more effective and efficient, and the end product was stronger as a result.

Patricia's daily practice consists of a twenty-minute meditation each morning and, sometimes, in the evening. She typically sits in a chair, and she now uses the unguided timer on Meditation Studio. Sometimes, when feeling restless, she uses her favorite meditation app—Meditation Studio, of course—for one of its many guided meditations. Her favorite go-to guided meditation is in the app's Confidence section and is called "Mountain Strength."

With the success of Meditation Studio and her podcast *Untangle*, Patricia has been asked to speak to groups more frequently. As with so many others, public speaking makes Patricia anxious. She made it a personal challenge to work on this by taking a presentation class that utilized a technique from the popular NPR storytelling podcast *The Moth*. The class required participants to perform live storytelling in a café in front of strangers, something Patricia originally didn't know was part of the program.

Patricia prepared her story with much anxiety, and when the day of her performance arrived, she almost left the café. Once again, her practice served her well. Through awareness of her feelings, she had the foresight to listen to the "Public Speaking" guided meditation in the Performance collection of Meditation Studio. After the meditation, she listened to a favorite song that pumped her up: "Girl Is on Fire" by Alicia Keys. These techniques allowed her to calm down and feel strong, resulting in a successful performance at the café that day.

Now that Patricia is an entrepreneur, the stresses are different, but equally, if not more, intense than in the corporate world. It's interesting to witness how far meditation has come in such a short time: the market is literally flooded with apps that teach meditation and keep people on track with their daily practice. She knows that every day she will get up and potentially be joined by another competitive company. Her practice is allowing her to persevere and stay focused on the company's mission: to share with the world that, although the mind is complicated, meditation doesn't have to be.

Jeffrey Walker, Vice Chairman of the United Nations Envoy's Office for Health Finance and Malaria

Philanthropist and chairman of the board of New Profit, Jeffrey Walker is an accomplished man in many spheres. He has an MBA from Harvard Business School and a bachelor's of science from the University of Virginia. For twenty-five years, Jeffrey was CEO and cofounder of CCMP Capital, the $12 billion successor to JPMorgan Partners, JPMorgan Chase's global private equity firm; vice chairman of JPMorgan Chase & Co.; and chairman of the JPMorgan Chase Foundation.

These days, Jeffrey serves as vice chairman of the United

Nations Envoy's Office for Health Finance and Malaria. He is also extremely active in the philanthropic world and serves on the boards of New Profit, Berklee College of Music, Morgan Library, Lincoln Center Film Society, the Miller Center, and the University of Virginia (UVA) Undergraduate Business School. Jeffrey is also cofounder and cochairman of the Quincy Jones Musiq Consortium, and chair of the Council of Foundations at UVA. He serves on the Visiting Committee at Harvard Business School and is on advisory boards at MIT, UCLA, UVA, Columbia, Brookings, and other institutions. In 2013, Jeffrey coauthored *The Generosity Network*, with Jennifer McCrea. The book shares new ways to approach fundraising for large and small nonprofit organizations.

You might also recognize Jeffrey from his popular TED talk about Jeffersonian Dinners. The talk gives the audience the motivation, inspiration, and tools to bring a group of diverse people together to focus on a single topic. The dinner starts with each participant sharing their background and preconceived thoughts on the topic, moves to an open forum, and ends with a call to action. What a concept!

Jeffrey credits his forty-three years of meditation practice for his ability to be present and aware during both exciting and stressful moments. He first meditated at the

University of Virginia in 1973—it was nighttime, the sky was full of stars: *So much space up there.* (Maybe a beer was involved, but just one!) He'd read about meditation before, and his psychology class had recently studied the practice of noticing the body. That night he sat in a field silently and meditated.

Nowadays, Jeffrey has a regular daily practice, but he also finds himself practicing throughout the day. When he finds a free moment, he may pause, close his eyes, and breathe for two minutes. Other times, he may choose to do other forms of meditation practice. It's fluid and depends on the day and how he is feeling.

Jeffrey shares that he found his daily practice especially helpful during the 9/11 tragedy. During this time, an "action" he took was to teach meditation to his employees and peers as a way of being in tune with the anxiety and uncertainty they were feeling. While at JPMorgan Chase, Jeffrey also led workshops with many of the leadership teams.

Meditation changed the way Jeffrey interacted with others, especially during business negotiations. He began to quickly notice when he was not listening well enough, or when there were too many thoughts rolling around in his mind. The skill of noticing is one piece; the next step is stopping yourself before you react—by simply becoming aware of your breath. Jeffrey also noticed habits changing in those who participated in his meditation workshops. "They are such smart people and want to be sure their peers know how smart they are. Their practice began to break that ego portion down, and associates began actually listening to each other better."

As a full-time philanthropist and someone who is generous with his time and wisdom, Jeffrey encourages us not only to cultivate a meditation practice, but to find passions in the nonprofit world and dig deep into them. In fact, Jeffrey would love to hear from you and is always willing to help you find yours.

chapter twelve

How Do I Maintain a Daily Practice?

· · · · ·

It's easy...but it's hard. It takes discipline, vulnerability, and help from those you live and work with.

You're already a successful leader, and you got where you are today because you set goals in life. Big surprise: setting a goal to meditate is no different. Like most things in life, you begin with the end in mind. What do you want your meditation practice to look like in three months, six months, and twelve months? Let's say it's to meditate at least twenty minutes per day. I'm probably not sharing anything you don't already know: set the goal and do it for twenty-one straight days—the amount of time proven to create a habit.

Some time ago, I took a three-year course called The

Strategic Coach, held in both Toronto and Chicago. The founder, Dan Sullivan, is a true creative visionary. He's created all sorts of tools for goal-setting, productivity, and idea generation. I'll never forget one of the first things I learned during the course, which actually had nothing to do with any of his tools.

The instructor was free-flowing us into the next part of our day and mentioned that a number of years ago, he was down on himself because he wanted to read more. But he never read at all. He wanted to, loved the idea of it, but just never did it! So, he decided to create a twenty-one-day habit: pick a book and read just one page of that book per day. And he did! As you might imagine, one page would often lead to two, which led to four, which led to a full chapter. Now he's an avid reader.

I love that story because, at the time, I felt the same way about reading. So, I made the same commitment and, like him, I've now become an avid reader, often reading up to three books at a time. It's also the method I used to write this book. As you may have noticed, I'm a first-time author. I committed to writing one page per day for at least twenty-one days. And that's what I did, with the one page often turning into many pages!

You can use this same philosophy for beginning your meditation practice, starting with one minute and gradually working your way up each day. To time your sitting, you can keep it simple and use a household timer, or, if it's easier, your smartphone's timer. (Just be sure to turn off all notifications before starting.)

Best-selling author Seth Godin sums it up when he says: "The habits we groove become who we are, one minute at a time. A small thing, repeated, is not a small thing."

There are also many meditation apps on the market. Some of my favorites are Meditation Studio, Headspace, and 10% Happier, all of which are subscription-based after a short trial period. I use an app called Insight Timer, which allows me to choose the duration of my meditation and different bell sounds to start and end any given session.

Research shows that just because you have the intention to form new habits does not mean you will necessarily stick with them. One of the first discussions in the Virginia Military Institute's Modern Warriorship class is about habit formation: how to start and keep a habit. Professor Matt Jarman has the cadets start with a fifteen-minute daily meditation when they wake and another five minutes before they start their homework. The key is tying the meditation to that schedule. For a true habit, no will-power is needed: a habit, once established, doesn't take any extra effort.

Research has proven that effective habit formation requires repetition and contextual cues, such as the same time of day and environment. Rewards are also important. With meditation, these are inherently intermittent. Sometimes you'll have lots of energy, other times just a regular calm.

Again, research shows that this is why people stay with the practice: if there were amazing benefits and experiences every time, our nature would be to stop, but because the benefits take time and are intermittent, we stick with it. A great example Matt uses is a comparison to running. When we run, there is a larger reason for doing it, usually better physical health. But, along the way, some runs are extremely easy, while others feel difficult. Yet, many stick with the routine because those intermittent, great-feeling runs make it all worth it!

As mentioned earlier, Chade-Meng Tan, an engineer at Google and their 107th employee, had a dream to change the world by utilizing meditation as a tool for a more mindful society. I'll share some great advice he has for keeping your meditation practice on track:

- Find a buddy and commit to a fifteen-minute conversation every week to discuss how you are doing with your practice and what has arisen in your life that relates to your practice.

- Try doing less. If your goal is twenty minutes per day, try just fifteen minutes, or ten minutes twice per day. You don't want the practice to become a burden, and you want to succeed.
- Commit to one mindful breath per day. Just one. Breathe in and breathe out mindfully, and your commitment is fulfilled. Anything additional you do beyond that is a bonus!
- Have the intention to meditate each day. Even one breath encourages you to do something simple that isn't time-consuming and is ultimately helpful in cultivating what will become a strong practice in the future.

As you grow your practice, be open, honest, and vulnerable. Talk to important people in your life about your goal, such as your significant other, spouse, kids, roommates, or coworkers. Share why you're starting your practice—it will benefit them as much as you—and let them know that you'll be sitting silently somewhere in your home or office for a set duration of time each day.

Ask for their help. More than likely they will be supportive, excited, and probably a bit curious, even if they give you a funny look at first, secretly thinking, *You're going to sit quietly for twenty minutes? There's so much we need to do! And remember that Netflix series we were binging? It's calling our name!* If they don't seem to be supportive, ask them why. Dig in with them and share what you've learned in this book: the science, the facts, and the stories of real-life people and leaders who have successfully incorporated the practice into their extremely busy lives.

chapter**thirteen**

Very Busy People with Consistent Daily Practices

· · · · ·

Too busy to meditate every day? It's more likely that you're too busy *not* to meditate. Check out what two of the most successful entrepreneurs in the world—best-selling author Tim Ferriss and Andrew Cherng of Panda Express—have to say on the subject.

Tim Ferriss, Author, Entrepreneur, and Public Speaker

Tim Ferriss is a successful entrepreneur, host of the top-ranking podcast *The Tim Ferriss Show*, and author of the best-selling books *The 4-Hour Workweek*, *The 4-Hour Body*, *The 4-Hour Chef*, *Tools of Titans*, and, most recently, *Tribe of Mentors*.

In *Tools of Titans,* Tim shares best practices from one hundred highly successful people interviewed on his podcast over the years. Those profiled are all world-class performers in different areas of life—business, athletics, writing, science, and so on—and he spends three to seven pages sharing each of their tactics, routines, and secrets of success. There was one theme across all one hundred individuals that Tim calls "The Most Consistent Pattern of All."

More than 80 percent of the world-class performers interviewed had some form of daily meditation or mindfulness practice. In the book, Tim concludes that one of the key benefits to starting your day by practicing focus through meditation when it *doesn't* matter, is that you can focus better later, when it really *does* matter!

Some might be afraid that a regular meditation practice will make them lose their edge, but the exact opposite occurs. Consistently, high achievers find they are able to perform at an even higher level than before because of the awareness and presence they have developed. The world starts to slow down. Tim interviewed a US Army general who spoke about soldiers being able to remain calm while "bullets were whizzing past their heads." With twenty minutes of consistent, daily meditation, they could take in what was happening around them at a higher level. It was like having the ability to look down on the battlefield, move the regiments around, and calmly execute a plan.

In the book, Tim shares the details of his personal practice, including how he initially committed to a daily practice. He started with an unwavering commitment to seven consecutive days without missing, comparing this to how "if your doctor prescribes a week of antibiotics and you only take the medication for three days, the infection isn't fixed and you're back to square one." If you need an accountability partner, he recommends finding a "buddy" to take the challenge with you, or utilizing a service like Coach.me or Stickk.com. His method was to complete the seven consecutive days before getting ambitious with length, starting with around ten minutes or so per day. "Start small and rig the game so you can win."

Once past the initial stages of creating the daily routine, Tim settled into a twenty-minute daily discipline. He started to notice that the first fifteen minutes of his practice were "letting the mud in the water settle," and the last five minutes felt the most beneficial. Compare this to weight lifting: the beginning reps are needed, but the last few reps are where you gain the real benefits. Tim goes on to explain that if you are spending 19.5 minutes of your meditation thinking about all the "important" things going on in your life, like to-do lists or a recent disagreement, you do not get an "F" in meditation. Just one second of noticing your mind wandering and bringing your attention back to your breath is a success. You are working that muscle. Some workouts will be better than others, but all will be beneficial. What's important to remember is this: "If you're getting frustrated, your standards are too high, or your sessions are too long."

The goal is not to completely silence your thoughts; it's to notice them. Noticing is awareness. Tim found that he began to bring his practice, cultivated over time, into real-life scenarios, stopping to pause and be thoughtful about his response, whereas before he would normally "react." For Tim, there is a big payoff: "When I meditate consistently, my reward is getting 30 percent to 50 percent more done in a day with 50 percent less stress. Because I've done a warmup in recovering from distraction."

Or in the words of Abraham Lincoln: "Give me six hours to chop down a tree, and I'll spend the first four sharpening the axe."

Andrew Cherng, CEO of Panda Express

Andrew Cherng immigrated to the United States when he was eighteen years old. Just seven years later, in 1973, he started his first restaurant. Now, Andrew oversees one of the largest Chinese-American fast-food chains in the United States, Panda Express. Andrew is a thoughtful leader who believes that every person is on their own personal journey.

I had the chance to speak with Andrew about his meditation practice, a tool that has been important for his leadership and personal life. But Andrew is quick to point out that he doesn't consider himself an expert on the topic. In fact, at times he struggles to maintain his daily practice. Even when the practice itself is a challenge, Andrew never loses sight of how important it is to stay in touch with your inner self. Andrew's ability to critique himself at a higher level speaks to his practice: he has high awareness and is working to go deeper. Like so many people, he sometimes struggles with that commitment and finds that, at this point in his life, "it just doesn't come naturally."

Anyone who has attempted a meditation practice can empathize with that sentiment. Yet, as a leader and a person, Andrew is committed to growth, and he explores many avenues for searching within, describing himself as "open to all kinds of techniques." We're all on a mindfulness journey, and we find ourselves at different points along the way throughout our lives. Currently, Andrew focuses on seeking out a variety of techniques that help him go inside himself, become a better person, and positively change something about himself on a regular basis. As leaders, those are some of the most important commitments we can make to ourselves, our teams, and those close to us.

In a story that has now become well known, Andrew once told a frazzled store manager to slow down and meditate before returning to work. In fact, Andrew looked him in the eyes and guided him through the process of meditating. Andrew wasn't doing this to prevent the nervous employee from embarrassing the company. He truly cares about the lives and well-being of his employees.

At Panda Express, the philosophy is that people can't do a good job at work if their lives are a mess. Employee well-being is promoted with monthly wellness seminars that teach nutrition, healthy habits, and meditation. Employees and managers are actively involved in each other's lives. Employees are encouraged to meditate, seek out new opportunities, and give back to the community. For Andrew, it's all about creating a business where people are helping one another live better lives.

Andrew approves of the "do nothing" characterization of meditation. "Do nothing is a very good way of saying it," he said. "Give something up to gain some wisdom."

chapter**fourteen**

Consider Taking a Silent Retreat

· · · · ·

I'm too busy. I could never do that. I've got no place in my home to meditate. I can't meditate at work! My significant other, spouse, or kids will bother me or think I'm nuts. It's a Buddhist ritual, and I'm not Buddhist. I can't sit still. I've tried, and I can't stop my thoughts. It's physically too painful to sit cross-legged. It's mentally too painful. I know, I've got to do it, and I'm not sure why I'm not.

These are many of the reasons I hear as to why people don't meditate. The bottom line, as we've already discussed, is that it comes down to creating a habit. I'm guessing many of you know all about creating habits: you got to where you are today because of good habits. You also know about commitment. Again, you've succeeded because you are committed, and you are accountable. Meditation is no different.

What's unlikely is that you have ever been given the following challenge to enhance your leadership skills: commit to a daily practice *and* take a silent meditation retreat. Why in the world would you do this? How would you find the time? You have so many commitments both in business and your personal life. But I know one thing about leaders: if it will improve their leadership skills or business results, they find the time. What if that thing would not only improve your leadership but your life skills? Would you find the time?

Taking a silent retreat is a tool I used to get started on the right note, providing a foundation to jumpstart my practice. It taught me the proper skills to successfully maintain a daily meditation practice. Each retreat gets me thinking at a deep level—no, deeper—even deeper! Have you been to therapy? I have. A silent retreat will not replace quality time with a trained professional, but what it did do is save me thousands of dollars and lots of time by gently bringing out deeper thoughts that I did not realize had been affecting me for years. Meditation and silent retreats allow me to practice how to simply *be* with those thoughts. Once I do so, I start to let go. Once I start to let go, I begin to be a better person to all of those around me, as well as myself.

So, here's my challenge to you and to all business leaders

who want to refine their awareness and presence deeply. Consider the potential of enhancing your practice with a silent meditation retreat. Yes, silent: no talking, no electronics, totally immersed in learning the practice and creating the habit.

Again, this may seem extreme, but if the result is that you become a *much* better person, isn't it worth it? If you're not doing it for yourself, how about doing it for those around you? Maybe it seems like a daunting experience, but, in actuality, almost every person I know returns from a silent retreat with renewed awareness, clarity, calmness, and energy. It's a very human experience, where instructors and participants treat you with compassion and encourage you to be kind to yourself as well. As for the time commitment, the inconvenience you and the others in your life will experience while you are away will *quickly* be overridden by these positive changes when you return.

Sharing the desire—or blind faith—to attend a silent retreat with your loved ones and coworkers can be intimidating. They may not understand the benefits of a retreat right away: how it will positively affect you and, as a result, them. They may not understand that you'll likely come back a better significant other, spouse, parent, family member, friend, coworker, leader: just an all-around better human being to those who are around you every day. Even if you're pretty great in these roles already, they will notice a different energy, awareness, and presence after your retreat.

Committing to a silent retreat is a bold investment in becoming your best self, and it pays off. The people in your life, the people that truly know you and care about you, *will* support you. Why wouldn't they? If there's hesitation, help them understand exactly what a meditation retreat is and the science behind its benefits.

You've already met Patricia Karpas, a successful businesswoman and one of *Forbes*'s ten world-renowned meditation tech experts. Recently Patricia attended her first seven-day silent retreat at the Shambhala Mountain Center approximately thirty minutes from Fort Collins, Colorado. The experience gave her even greater clarity, and she feels more grounded. She says the retreat made a measurable difference and allowed her to uncover some of the layers of "stuff" that she has going on in her head— as we all do!

During the retreat, Patricia found her awareness was heightened. She said, "Your truth becomes clearer. You get to a deeper place and stay in that place. You accept that suffering happens close to you and far away, and as you practice, you fall apart less and less. The more you practice, the more you are creating the world you want to live in."

Both Jeffrey Walker and Andrew Cherng, whom you also met earlier, attend and derive great benefit from silent retreats. Jeffrey attends several a year and finds they greatly enhance his meditation practice.

My own first retreat experience was challenging, but I found myself settling into the practice and awareness by the end of the day. My next and subsequent retreats were seven to ten days in length. I found they helped to hone my practice of awareness: full presence in this moment, right here, right now. The first few days, I would notice lots of surface chatter in my head. Midway through, I would start to notice a calming taking place—deeper thoughts arising and disappearing, as I noticed and returned to my breath. Coming back from a retreat, I'd find myself less anxious, calmer, and more present.

I've completed five seven-day and one ten-day silent retreats over the past three years, and each time I return, my presence and awareness are strengthened. My intention is to take two seven-to-ten-day silent retreats per year to continue to work my awareness muscle.

How Long Should I Go For?

The duration of a silent retreat can vary from months and years—don't worry: that's not what we will be focused on—to seven-days, three-days, or just one-day long. Based on my personal experience, my recommendation is a four- or seven-day retreat. It may seem overwhelming to imagine this duration of silence, but I speak from experience, and, although all retreats are valuable, the seven-day and ten-day lengths were most valuable to me. It's also a lot simpler than you might think. While the vacations you normally take might be packed with activities and socializing, a silent retreat is true mind-and-body rejuvenation. This time frame allows for three distinct stages to occur:

1. **The Beginning**: An ease-in period where you are getting settled and are still at the "surface" of your thoughts and your life. It's crucial to give yourself time to work past this stage and go deeper.

2. **The Middle**: This phase brings more depth, as your mind begins to realize, for instance, that an argument you had with your significant other really doesn't matter. New thoughts and emotions begin to surface, many of which have been buried for years. Other thoughts may include groundbreaking ideas, new ways to look at challenges you've been facing, and a

feeling of embracing each waking moment, whether "good" or "bad," with love and respect.

3. **The End:** An ease-out period where you begin to realize that the retreat is ending. The surface thoughts begin to come back, you slowly begin to prepare to speak, and you get ready to carry this amazing feeling back into your day-to-day life.

Any amount of time that you can dedicate to mindfulness is valuable, so start with what is comfortable for you. In my experience, there's a positive correlation between the amount of time you can invest and your results. Whichever you choose, seven-day, four-day, and one-day silent retreats follow similar daily agendas.

What Should I Expect at a Silent Retreat?

When you arrive, the retreat will start gradually. You'll meet your fellow retreat participants, have dinner, share why you're there, and begin practicing with short sessions of sitting and walking. There will be some stretching and yoga mixed in to keep your body fresh. You'll eat amazing, healthy meals.

As the retreat gets underway, you'll have plenty of opportunity to ask questions to clarify anything you might be confused about. A typical day starts at 7:00 a.m. with breakfast, followed by a sitting meditation at 8:00 a.m. The first few days are a mixture of instruction and wisdom talks. On the third day, the instruction and wisdom talks gradually decrease, eventually being replaced by total silence from the instructors and participants.

I have found this to be the most impactful part of a retreat. By this point, I've had the opportunity to "let go" of my normal routines and habits—the tasks and obligations of day-to-day life—and I really settle in. For me, this is when most of the surface chatter at the front of my brain begins to dissipate and deeper feelings start to arise. For some, these deeper feelings can be beautiful, painful, or a mixture of both. I've witnessed numerous retreat participants burst out laughing as well as break down crying during a meditation session—and I've done both!

For the next three to four days, your awareness strengthens, and you start to notice little things you likely overlook during your daily routine. Life around you becomes a bit more vibrant, and details catch your attention. During one retreat, I noticed that a woman who was seated in front of me for the entire week wore her hair up in a bun most days. After most sitting sessions, I would open my eyes, see her hair bun, and think of my daughter, Frances, who often wears her hair the same way. It brought me to tears of happiness on more than one occasion. Simply seeing a stranger's hair bun made me cry. So simple—but that's the power of high-level awareness.

During completely silent days, signs are held up to indicate what the next activity is: sitting, walking, tea and a snack, yoga or stretching, and meal time are all common prompts. If a participant has questions, they are always able to get the attention of a teacher and write them a note, which will be promptly answered. Each day has a ninety-minute break following lunch, which gives you time to rest or take a walk.

Yes, the retreat is both physically and mentally tiring. I've sometimes found it difficult to sleep during retreats and have heard similar feedback from other participants. In this setting, lack of sleep often takes on a dreamlike quality: it is positively different from the "not sleeping" feeling we are accustomed to back home.

On the sixth day, the mood begins to change slightly. The instructors start slowly by doing a short wisdom talk. You'll notice the signs used for silent communication give way to verbal instruction. This is part of the process for slowly coming out of silence. You can feel the mixture of emotions in the room of fifty-plus participants: everything from excitement to anxiety to dread.

The next instruction is usually to pair up with another participant, where you will be given a subject or question to ask each other, which you answer by whispering. This is followed by speaking softly, followed by normal volume. My experience is usually that my voice has weakened, and it is difficult to get my words out. The muscle hasn't been worked for seven days, and it's not used to that. It takes a little bit of warming up, so you'll start by whispering, speaking softly, and then returning to normal volume.

The day closes, and that evening the meditation space is turned into a wonderful celebration with a healthy meal for all participants. The complete strangers you have been with for seven days, mostly not talking, suddenly feel like close friends. You've seen them throughout the week, and, because of the heightened awareness you have been gaining, you've noticed their habits and personal intricacies. Whether you're an introvert like me or an extrovert, it's a special moment to dine together, learn about each other, and finally speak!

The next morning, before departing, the group sits for one more silent meditation. After the meditation, the group sits in a large circle and writes haikus about their experience on a notecard. Many participants' haikus are creative, fun, uplifting, and emotional. I've never been good at stuff like that, so I usually keep it simple and write a short phrase such as, "Grateful for this gift." Because the retreat *is a gift* you give not only to yourself, but also to your loved ones, the people you work with, and the world around you.

What Does an Extended Retreat Do for You, Your Brain, and Your Thoughts?

For some, going on that first retreat is scary. It was for me, too. While there, I was without the usual entertainment and activities that distract me. I was left alone with my mind: its wisdom and calm, speed and confusion. What I saw was shocking at first, but as time went on, I adopted a friendly, kind, and often humorous attitude toward myself, realizing the real importance—or lack thereof—of things like how my wife loads the dishwasher, or who doesn't respond to my email within twenty-four hours.

Imagine a glass jar filled with water with some mud stirred into it. That's most of our brains: there's a lot swirling around up there. Imagine looking through the jar. You can't see through it, and you certainly wouldn't want to drink out of it. Imagine the jar untouched for a few days. It's still murky, but less so than before. You look through the jar and start to see through it a bit, although not very clearly. Imagine the jar untouched for a few more days. The mud is settling quite a bit. You can see more clearly when looking through the jar. You could even take a sip of the water without tasting any of the mud.

A retreat does this to the mind. It allows us to go deeper and let go of struggles. It allows simplicity in. Time is needed to clear the mind. Building on a retreat, daily meditation helps keep the water in the jar clear, the mud settled. We learn to be more aware and present. We make friends with ourselves and our emotions, and learn to be on stable ground as we experience life's ebbs and flows.

chapter fifteen

The *do**nothing***
Leadership Retreat

· · · · ·

Be bold! Take the leadership challenge by
starting with a silent meditation retreat!

While writing this book, I received a great deal of feedback from fellow business leaders encouraging me to organize a leadership-focused silent retreat. I heard this enough that I made the commitment to follow through. Like me, these colleagues were interested in sharing the powerful connection that exists among leaders who have all committed to going on a retreat and developing a daily practice. Details about the official *donothing* Leadership Retreat can be found at the *donothing* website: www.donothingbook.com.

If you attend a *donothing* Leadership Retreat, you'll be meeting other like-minded leaders with whom you will form strong bonds. Amazingly strong connections are formed while in silence!

The retreat is specifically intended to help leaders lead better: to be more in tune with their employees, customers, vendors, the community, and themselves. The retreat will give those who have a "command and control" executive style the opportunity to learn skills that they can incorporate in their lives to become better aware of and collaborate more fully with their employees.

The retreat might be a little different than what you expect. The four days are spent both sitting and doing other activities. You'll be learning to walk, eat, listen, and even rest mindfully: learning what it's like to tune into your sense perceptions, so as to become more aware of your body, your feelings, and your thoughts. And while full silence will be maintained for about a day and a half, the four-day retreat won't be completely silent.

Here's what to expect:

Day 1: You'll arrive and settle in, and we'll gather to set the stage for our time together. We'll introduce ourselves, enjoy dinner, have a short wisdom talk, and meditate.

Day 2: We'll start the day with instruction and meditation,

followed by breakfast and connecting. After lunch, we'll settle into silence. Our afternoon will include instruction, walking, stretching practice, meditation, and wisdom talks.

Day 3: The day will begin with instruction, meditation, and breakfast. After a period of sitting, walking, and stretching practice, there will be lunch and time to relax. Our afternoon will consist of instruction, small breakout groups for questions (with a special exception from silence), meditation, and wisdom talks.

Day 4: Our last day begins with instruction, meditation, and breakfast. We'll slowly come out of silence in the morning, followed by a group share. We'll enjoy a final lunch together before departing.

The retreat's benefits include the following:

- Four days unplugged—yes, this is a highlight!
- Learning mindfulness techniques from a senior meditation facilitator
- Connecting with other like-minded leaders
- Discovering how to bring mindfulness into your leadership and your life
- Soaking in the surroundings' inspiring energy
- Enjoying delicious locally prepared cuisine
- Private accommodations

Having given you the details, I'd like to share a little more background on why writing this book has become so important to me. Starting with my own meditation journey and from the depth of research on the topic, I know that mindful leadership is a truly transformative tool: for our personal leadership, for those we lead, and for those closest to us.

There are millions of leaders in this world. If just one thousand leaders take this challenge, I believe we can positively affect the lives of one million people. It starts with those closest to the leaders: their family members, friends, and community members. They will also impact the way their direct reports lead and manage. From there, consider the impact these people will have on how *their* friends and family members change their lens on the world and, in turn, enhance the lives of those close to them. Then there's the effect you, your direct reports, and those family members will have on every person they come into contact with on a daily basis: the coffee barista, the cashier at the grocery store, the server at the restaurant...

The goal of *donothing* is to change one million lives, and we will accomplish this if just one thousand leaders take this challenge. Committing to a meditation practice and taking a *donothing* Leadership Retreat will be the most rewarding leadership challenge you'll ever take. Take some time to envision yourself as a mindful leader. How could taking this challenge evolve your leadership? What will it mean to *donothing*? I've thought about it, and I have a clear vision for the impact this can have on the world four years from now. I hope you'll join me.

donothing Vision Statement

In March 2017, I attended a workshop through the Small Giants Community called "The Journey." During the workshop, we spent a day at ZingTrain, one of Zingerman's family of companies described earlier. At ZingTrain, we spent time creating a vision of the future for something important to us. I've done this exercise many times in the past, most notably with my personal 2026 vision and imageOne's 2026 Vision. I was just completing the first draft of this book and was inspired to create the *donothing* 2021 vision. Here it is:

It's 04/04/2021 and I'm blown away that the donothing book and retreats have taken on a life of their own. In the first twelve months, the book, donothing, started slowly with a small group of entrepreneurs and leaders who embraced it. Over the next twelve months, popularity began to pick up rapidly, with sales of ten thousand books. In 2019, 10 percent of those who read the book attended a donothing Leadership Retreat: one thousand people! Every year saw the numbers continue to multiply. We just surpassed our "one million lives affected" goal, as quantified by one thousand leaders in the world who have taken the challenge and, as a result, have greater awareness and presence with their teams.

*Talking about and taking on a meditation practice is common these days, thanks to all the trailblazers and advocates before me. I remember speaking with people back in 2017 about the idea of taking a retreat, and, for the most part, it was a foreign concept that was difficult for people to wrap their heads around. As business, technology, and priorities have changed over the last five years, new mindsets have opened up. What started in early 2018 as a simple retreat with thirty people, many of whom I had to personally cajole to join me at the first do**nothing** Leadership Retreat, quickly grew.*

With the simple book as the original springboard to understanding the benefits and science that quantify leadership and business results, we now have a small team of ten people who have developed a curriculum for others to set up and lead the retreat around the world. Distance and geography are not an issue, as over the past five years we have become closer and more interconnected than ever through technology and ease of travel.

We have a roster of trained and qualified facilitators to lead the retreats, and we are finding that leaders are making this an annual event, much like the annual industry conferences or business-group meetings they attend. Something that we didn't expect, but is now happening, is that leaders are including the retreat as a "benefit" for their teams, giving them time off and paying for them to attend.

The do**nothing** Family Retreats started because so many of the attendees of the do**nothing** Leadership Retreats asked us to create something for couples and families. We listened, and now many of those who have attended the do**nothing** Leadership Retreat are coming back with their significant others and children.

I'm humbled. I always felt that business could be conducted differently, and I'm proud that I let my "light shine" thanks to the encouragement from so many people, starting with a simple statement by one of my closest mentors, Michele McHall, while taking her journey: "Let your light shine, Rob..."

chapter**sixteen**

Discovering Retreats and Other Resources

• • • • •

The *donothing* Leadership Retreat is designed to serve entrepreneurs and business leaders, deepening their meditation practice to improve their professional and personal lives. If the dates don't fit your schedule, don't be discouraged. There are many wonderful retreat facilities around the world, and that's how I started my journey.

Meditation's benefits, like those of almost any positive activity such as exercise, increase over time and with consistent application. Just as athletes go through a period of intensive training before a competition, the concentration and intensity of a retreat reinforces and multiplies meditation's benefits. This isn't just speculation. In their book *Altered Traits: How Meditation Changes Your Mind, Brain, and Body,* Pulitzer Prize-winning psychologist Daniel

Goleman and neurology researcher Richard Davidson, founder of the Center for Healthy Minds at the University of Wisconsin, cite numerous studies showing that retreats further increase and enhance meditation's ability not only to summon but to sustain attention.

A retreat can be transformative. Here's what Congressman Tim Ryan of Ohio says about the effects of his first meditation retreat in 2008:

"I came out of the 2008 retreat with a whole new way of relating with what was going on in the world. And like any good thing that a congressman finds—a new technology, a new policy idea—immediately I said, 'How do we get this out there?'

"I've seen it transform classrooms. I've seen it heal veterans. I've seen what it does for individuals who have chronic stress and how it has helped their body heal itself. I wouldn't be willing to stick my neck out this far if I didn't think mindfulness can really help shift the country."

Starting and committing to a daily practice is a first giant step. However, I really urge those who find daily practice to be of benefit to attend a longer retreat. You really will be glad you did.

Here is a list of some centers and organizations to start your search.

Menla

Located two and a half hours from New York City, deep in the Catskill Mountains, Menla is a retreat, spa, and resort with meditation retreats that draw on Tibetan wisdom sciences.
http://menla.us/

Spirit Rock

Spirit Rock is an insight meditation center located in the secluded hills of Woodacre, California. Their retreats focus on the teachings of the Buddha, mindfulness, and loving-kindness meditation.
https://www.spiritrock.org/

Shambhala Mountain Center

Offering more than one hundred programs annually, Shambhala Mountain Center is a beautiful retreat located in the Colorado Rockies. Their practices span an array of ideologies and experience levels.
https://www.shambhalamountain.org/

Omega Institute

A well-known health and wellness organization, Omega Institute hosts thousands of people a year at their mindfulness retreats and programs. Omega has locations in New York, California, and Costa Rica.
https://eomega.org/mindfulness

Insight Meditation Society

Situated in the quiet woods of central Massachusetts, Insight Meditation Society is one of the oldest meditation retreat centers in the Western world. The center's primary focus is retreat programming, offering a variety of retreat lengths, practices—with a focus on mindfulness—and teachers.
http://www.dharma.org/

Vallecitos Mountain Retreat Center

Vallecitos offers retreats in a wild natural environment, located on a ranch in New Mexico's Tusas Mountains. It provides an intimate group setting for your retreat, with a maximum of forty guests and diverse teachings.
http://www.vallecitos.org/

University of Massachusetts MBSR Retreats

Retreats led by MBSR (Mindfulness-Based Stress Reduction program) certified teachers take place at several retreat centers around the world and offer a range of practices. The University of Massachusetts Center for Mindfulness offers a list of upcoming retreats and recommended retreat centers.

http://www.umassmed.edu/cfm/training/retreats/

Additional Resources: Meditation Apps

There has been a tremendous explosion of meditation apps in just the last couple of years. As I've already mentioned, some of my favorites are Meditation Studio, Headspace, and 10% Happier, all of which are subscription-based after a short trial period. I also use an app called Insight Timer, which allows me to choose the duration of my meditation and a different bell sound to start and end any given session. Other popular meditation apps include Muse and Apple's 2017 App of the Year, Calm. Also, here's a reminder that an app including Reggie Ray's guided instructions on posture can be found at Sounds True: http://www.soundstrue.com/store/the-seven-points-of-posture-1989.html.

Additional Resources: Meditation Research

The earlier chapter on scientific studies of meditation just scratched the surface. According to Daniel Goleman and Richard Davidson in their book *Altered Traits:* "In the 1970s, when we began publishing our research on meditation, there were just a handful of scientific articles on the topic. At last count there numbered 6,838 such articles, with a notable acceleration of late. For 2014 the annual number was 925, in 2015 the total was 1,098, and in 2016 there were 1,113 such publications in the English language scientific literature."

Those interested can keep up with the latest scientific research into the benefits of meditation on the following websites:

- https://centerhealthyminds.org/: Richard Davidson and the Center for Healthy Minds, University of Wisconsin, Madison
- https://www.mindandlife.org/: Mind and Life Institute
- https://nccih.nih.gov/: National Center for Complementary and Integrative Health
- http://ccare.stanford.edu/: Center for Compassion and Altruism Research and Education, Stanford University
- http://mbct.com/: Mindfulness-based cognitive therapy

- http://www.umassmed.edu/cfm/: Judson Brewer and the Center for MBSR (Mindfulness-Based Stress Reduction)
- https://www.resource-project.org/en/home.html/: researcher Tania Singer
- http://www.amishi.com/lab/: researcher Amishi Jha
- http://saronlab.ucdavis.edu/: researcher Clifford Saron
- https://www.psych.ox.ac.uk/research/mindfulness/: Oxford Mindfulness Centre
- http://marc.ucla.edu/: UCLA Mindful Awareness Research Center

Acknowledgments

· · · · ·

I would like to start by thanking you, the reader, for taking the time to read this book. This is humbling for me, and I've thought about you throughout the entire process. My focus was to provide you with value, to be respectful of your time and mindshare, and to keep it simple. Writing this book was a passionate pursuit and challenge, and many people have supported me over the past fourteen months. It's emotional for me to think about!

Thank you to my wife, Emily. I shared this idea with her in December 2016, and, as usual, she listened intently and gave me wise advice. In this case, it was to go for it. Sounds simple, but I knew this was going to be a challenge that would last a year or more. That part was certainly true! I started by writing a few pages in my office in Harbor Springs, Michigan, where we have a second home, and reading them to Emily. Being an English major, she had a good number of corrections, but thought the content was on point and encouraged me to keep going, so I did. As always, her support through the ebbs and flows of the process was unwavering. I'm so fortunate to have such a spirited soul as my wife. I love you!

Our children, William and Frances, were always interested in how it was going and shared with me their excitement about reading it when it was completed. That's saying a lot considering that they don't have a lot of "spare time" for extra reading, what with work and school obligations. Both graduated in 2017, William from college, Frances from high school. Both are now officially away from home. It's been an interesting transition, one that my meditation has been helpful with. I'm so proud of them, miss them so much it hurts my heart, and I love them so much.

At imageOne's 2017 Annual Planning Session, our team all shared something we would do in 2017 that was "scary." This was my "scary." It has been incredibly challenging and rewarding.

I elicited a number of test readers throughout the process: some I knew well, some I didn't, some who loved the topic, and others who were skeptical. Paul Spiegelman was the first reader of my first draft, and he didn't hold back. Paul, thank you for your tough love. It was just what I needed.

The next wave of readers included Jim Schell, Noah Siegel, Gino Wickman, Bo Burlingham, Aly Waibel, Rachel Reardon, Anese Cavanaugh, Jim Colosi, and my best friend, Joel Pearlman. Of course, Emily Dubé was asked, and obliged, to read the manuscript on more than one occasion! And, Emmy Georgeson, your unique ability to listen and help me construct my ideas was invaluable. Thank you all for your mixture of thoughtful feedback and encouragement. It meant the world to me. I listened and made many changes because of your wisdom.

My parents, Carol Rozich and Bob Dubé, have always been there for me, and I'll always be grateful to them. Thank you for raising me the way you did. I would not want a thing to be different: it shaped me into the person I am today. Many times, they asked, "How's the book going? I'd love to read it." Hint, hint... But, since they know me so well, I made them wait for the book to be published. To their significant others, Bob Rozich and Ruth Dubé: thank you for your curiosity and support! My sister, Michelle—you've always been there without judgement. I'm so grateful for that and for your support with anything I set out to do in my life. You are an inspiration to so many! My brother Drew was incredibly helpful, curious, and creative throughout the process. He helped me follow up on emails to the amazing people I was able to interview, as well as securing a TEDx talk about *donothing*. I'm so proud of you for the journey you're on and excited for the day I can help you the way you've helped me.

Thank you to Hamsa Daher for giving me the opportunity to speak on this topic at the 2016 Small Giants Summit in Denver. That talk and the feedback that followed were the seed that sprouted into this book. And, on top of that, you introduced me to Jillian Rodriguez, my first editor. Jillian, your curiosity and willingness to learn, your gentle approach to suggestions, and your dedication to my project have all been a gift to me. The subsequent blogs for *Thrive Global* and *Forbes*, on top of your assistance with my social media presence, have been so much fun. You totally "get it." I'll miss working with you! Thank you to Tom Lane, who helped me do the final edit on the book. Tom, I had no idea that I would be meeting an amazing editor but an even more amazing person. I enjoyed every interaction we had together and look forward to working with you on my next project!

Thank you to the team at imageOne. You've all been so supportive of all my endeavors over the years, and this was no different. I'm humbled to work with such a special group of people.

Thank you to Jeffery Kaftan, *Jiggggy*! You inspire and challenge me with care and love. I'm more focused than ever because of you and I treasure our friendship.

Thank you to David Mammano for encouraging me to join his "Avanti Mastermind Group." The group—Rochelle Lisner, Kelly Hatfield, Andrew Harrison, and Mike Caceci—challenged me each month in just the right way. I listened intently and took action. What started with a basic manuscript when we began meeting turned into...

- A published manuscript
- A live website
- A retreat
- Regular social media contributions
- A biweekly blog with *Thrive Global* and a weekly one with *Forbes*
- Numerous speaking invitations including a TEDx talk

Of course, I believe things happen for a reason, and, David, your nudge was no accident. You have been an invaluable resource, but more importantly a great friend.

Thank you to Patricia Karpas for allowing me to interview you for the book. The unanticipated outcome of that interview is a new and extremely special friend. You are thoughtful, caring, deep, feeling, driven, and, most importantly, one of the best listeners I have ever met. Our dialogue during this process has helped me tremendously, and I'm excited to have you as part of my life.

Thank you to Paul Spiegelman, David Mammano, Kelly Hatfield, and again Patricia Karpas for inviting me on your podcasts. I felt they were all quality interviews, which says so much about the type of people you are. Paul, your interview really got me to dig deep, and I appreciate that: it translated into making this a better book.

Thank you to Gino Wickman for inspiring me, for mentoring me in the book writing and publishing process, and most of all for being an amazing friend. Congratulations on everything you've built. Stay focused!

Thank you to Bo Burlingham for striking up a conversation with me in line at Zingerman's in 2008. You've become such a great friend and special person in my life. You are the most curious person I've ever met. But more importantly, you are kind, thoughtful, and humble. You're a hero to so many of us in the entrepreneurial community, yet you don't see yourself that way at all. That lesson in humility is one I think about often.

Thank you to Joel Pearlman, my brother by another mother. Thanks for being you. How did I get so lucky to meet you in grade school? It makes no sense! And the fact that we are still together after all these years, through the ups and downs and flow of life, watching you grow alongside me, helping me to see the other side of things and different perspectives, and serving as my truth serum—it's amazing. I love you!

About the Author

· · · · ·

From Blow Pops to *Forbes*'s Best Small Companies: Rob Dubé started selling Blow Pops out of his locker in high school and is now president and cofounder of imageOne, which was ranked on the 2017 list of *Forbes*'s Top 25 Small Giants: America's Best Small Companies.

Throughout Rob's twenty-six years of experience, he has developed an unwavering passion for delivering extraordinary experiences that positively impact the lives of his team members, the goals of their customers, and the fabric of the community. This unique approach to business has driven the company to success in its industry and acknowledgment as a top workplace. imageOne is the leading organization in document lifecycle management and is well known as an exceptional company, receiving local and national recognition for its strong focus on culture.

Rob is an avid meditator of thirteen years and founder/organizer of the *donothing* Leadership Retreat. He is a contributor to *Forbes*, *Thrive Global*, and *EO Octane*.

Made in the USA
Columbia, SC
29 June 2018